THE SLY MIND

THE SLY MIND

THE STRUCTURE OF HUMAN MIND, AND ITS REFUSAL TO BE CONTROLLED
[THE MISCHIEVOUS IMP]

DR. TALIB KAFAJI

PARTRIDGE

To order additional copies of this book, contact
Toll Free 800 101 2657 (Singapore)
Toll Free 1 800 81 7340 (Malaysia)
orders.singapore@partridgepublishing.com

www.partridgepublishing.com/singapore

Contents

Introduction vii

1. The Landscape of the Mind 1

2. The Nature of Thought 5

3. The Mysteries of the Mind 9

4. Our Conscious and Unconscious Mind 17

5. The Power of the Unconscious Mind 25

6. Ghost In the Machine 32

7. Establishing the Paradigm of Our Thoughts 36

8. The Mind - Body Relationship 41

9. The Biology of Thoughts 45

10. Neuroplasticity 51

11. Mirror Neurons 59

12. If You Resist, It Will Persist: The Nature of the Sly Mind ... 68

13. Culture and Mass Delusions 73

14. Left Brain vs. Right Brain 77

15. The Power of Suggestion 82

16. The Negative Frame of Mind 90

17. Intrusive Thoughts: OCD 102

18. Pathological Thinking 110

19. The Energy of Thoughts 116

20. The Child Riding an Elephant 125

21. The Role of Psychology in Correcting Erroneous Thoughts 131

22. The Peaceful Mind and Creative Thoughts 142

23. How to Acquire A Super Mind.. 146

24. How to Master Your Mind 150

25. Brain Food 158

Conclusions... 163

References 169

Introduction

Why is it necessary to understand the mind? The answer is simple and logical. Happiness and suffering are states of mind. If we want to be free from suffering and enjoy true happiness, we need to possess a thorough understanding of the mind and how to control it. No other way can definitely improve our quality of life, both now and in the future.

The human mind and the dynamic of thinking are the most important topics that need to be explored, investigated and studied today. Because, all of our troubles and miseries come from the thinking process, which often is not under our control. The mind is its own control independent of us, and has brought all of the suffering to individuals, because, the mind by its nature is inclined to be negative and illogical.

Birds, zebras, or ants live by their instincts. We are living at the mercy of our uncontrollable mind, which often is working against us under the pretext of saving us from danger. Sadly, the job of the mind is not to make us happy; the job of the mind is to protect us. It is designed for hunting and gathering, not modern life. Thus, it acts as if we are in the forest hunting animals and the animals are running after us. Therefore, fear is our basic instinct.

This book will explore all the aspects of our mind and how it affects us. Is there any hope mankind can regulate the mischievous imp, let alone stop it? We cannot stop our thoughts. The thoughts that we face in our daily lives – depression, anxiety, obsessive thinking, irrational thoughts – can be regulated, if we can master such skills. Otherwise, we live with such disturbances for the rest of our lives.

As far as our perceptions, we perceive the world through our five senses. The information we have about the outside world is through the windows of the five senses. But our senses are limited, so perhaps it is not reality we perceive. For example, we see people in a dream and exactly the same people in real life. Which is real, the dream or the real event? How can we differentiate between the dream and reality, or between imagination and reality, and know our perception is not deceiving us? Maybe our reality is based on false perceptions. All of these inquiries are investigated in this book. We may not be able to come up with any satisfactory answers, but the most important thing is to challenge our traditional thinking about what reality means.

Furthermore, sometimes it appears our mind is beyond our control. So who is controlling it? For example, sometimes you give a command to your mind, but it will go in the opposite direction from where you want it to go. This can result in serious mental and emotional disturbances, because the "control room" is not listening to what we want it to do. Our brain is acting independently of us. When you have obsessive thoughts, you do not like the thought, but it keeps appearing in spite of your refusal. So who is in control?

The more you do not want these thoughts to appear, the more they tend to persist. Why is that? Who is asking the thought to appear, while you are telling the thought not to? The thought has established itself in the unconscious mind, and it takes tremendous time and energy to reprogram the mind.

Metaphorically speaking, when it comes to the dynamic of our thoughts, we look like a child who is riding an elephant. Psychology has been investigating such serious phenomena. The core of human suffering is the inability to control the mind. It is like a child riding an elephant. The child is us and the elephant is our thoughts. The elephant is wandering around aimlessly, making the child frightened, anxious and helpless. That is exactly what is happening to us.

It can take all the joy out of life, and make our lives, at the very least, unpleasant. So then, what is the point of living? Is it to suffer? Animals do not suffer, as they live by their instincts. At least, perhaps they suffer less than we do.

When you ask people if they are happy, they may say they are occasionally. But most of the time the mind brings unwanted thoughts, which nag our brain, and gnaws at our soul. One of my patients told me he worries over nothing, and his life is wonderful. He has a loving wife, three lovely children, a great job, is very healthy, and has a great income. But something keeps telling him that something bad will happen. Rationally, he knows nothing will happen to him, but his sly mind brings disturbing thoughts, which make him feel anxious and depressed. He questions who brings disturbing thoughts to his mind, since he does not want them. Ironically, he does not find an answer to his dilemma, and his life keeps going, loaded with fears and worries.

It's the human conundrum. Modern psychology has determined we have a conscious and an unconscious mind. Normally we store unwanted material in the unconscious mind, as these materials tend to be bothersome. On the contrary, we do not store the good materials. When we store the bad materials, they creep into the conscious mind without our awareness, and become a dark thick cloud hanging over us. That is not unusual, the majority of people have a negative frame of mind, and struggle with that most of their lives. If they engage in therapeutic treatment, they may reach a state of realization that these thoughts are destructive, and have to be regulated.

Humans are endowed with this mischievous imp, our sly mind. This is why, from the start, we are doomed with negative inclinations. Basically we constantly suffer from this dark cloud. It seems there is no end to human predicaments from internal conflicts, and their manifestations. The disturbing materials come to mind without our permission, and they keep coming even if we scream day and night. The disturbing thoughts become an independent entity, with a life of their own.

We have to be aware when disturbing thoughts manifest, we should not believe them; they are a figment of our imagination. Our mind is our number one enemy, and that may give hope that we are not slaves to our unfounded unconscious thoughts.

First, we have to understand how our mind becomes abusive to us, and why it becomes the source of our disturbances, and why logic does not work with our mind. Nothing may work against our mind. The more pressure you put on the mind not to bring the dark cloud, the more it comes, and paralyzes your thinking. These are all legitimate questions, and philosophers as well as psychologists have wrestled with them for centuries. Perhaps this book may provide some answers, or some means of how to be in control of your mind.

A formidable question, unanswered since man first walked the earth, is why is the mind enamored with negative thoughts, and tends to forget positive experiences, yet holds onto the negative ones?

The evolutional psychology and Carl Jung have given us a glimpse of why we are negative by nature. Our ancestors had a troubled life; from illness, to cold, to heat, to animal attacks. The troubling events have become stored in our unconscious mind. Thus, we are negative and disturbed people, because the unconscious mind brings it to the surface of our consciousness, so we can be careful and safe. But why are we paying for the misery of our ancestors?

From the mind's perspective, it wants to keep us safe and away from danger. But the mind often exaggerates danger, or there is no danger at all. This is why life is not always serene. This book will give you an understanding of the dynamic of your mind, and give you the practical tools to manage your mind and make your life a meaningful journey worth living. Undoubtedly, sincerity in attempting to develop oneself and live a happy life, requires some energy, dedication, and paying close attention to what enters your mind.

Dr.Talib Kafaji
February, 2016
Marrakech, Morocco

Chapter One

The Landscape of the Mind

As a man thinks in his heart, so he can be. – James Allen

The mind is pattern-oriented when it comes to daily activities. With this pattern recognition, our mind creates, stores, and recognizes patterns. The mind also can and does create its own patterns, and may later recognize them when presented with related data.. Raw data is received by the brain, and is quickly digested into recognized patterns.

How do we understand the mind? It performs so many functions; it is a confusing mess. How many times have you experienced mixed thoughts, feelings, ideas, solutions, and memories, all clamoring for some mental real estate, while you are trying to stay focused on something else? Cognitive psychologists have tried to make sense out of this for many years. We need to understand the nature of our thoughts and how they operate automatically. Research by Daniel Kahneman has shown the following categories of thinking:

1. The engaged mind. You have immersed yourself in the task at hand, and you are happy when you are engaged, because that removes worry from you. This is what we need in daily life. Movement meditation teaches people how to engage in every single minute. Certainly, that keeps us focused, and takes away distractions.

2. The automatic mind. We are swimming in the stream of automatic thoughts and memories, which come to us effortlessly. All these thoughts are determined by internal conflict, instincts, perceptions or prior learning. They help us, and are essential for our survival, but they are also full of misinformation,

distortions and bias. We basically copy the thoughts of yesterday or last month or last year; thus on a daily basis, almost 90% of our thoughts are automatic. This is why we do not have creative thoughts, because the margin for creativity is so limited.

Unfortunately, automatic thoughts tend to be mostly negative and troubling, and often are so strong that we cannot stay engaged. Thus, the automatic mind can become an unbearable place from which we try to escape. Automatic thoughts remove us from the here and now, and make us anxious and fearful. It is like autopilot; we have no control, and feel helpless in the face of automatic thoughts.

In obsessive thinking, the automatic thought makes life sheer misery. Basically, it takes away all joy from life; thus, we have to design therapeutic techniques to manage or control automatic thoughts. Unfortunately, most of us are addicted to our automatic thoughts, whether we like or not. They tend to dominate life, and give us a dizzy mind.

3. <u>The analytic mind</u>. Our mind works in broad categories, with most of it automatic thoughts. However, the analytical mind can also observe, reflect, solve, plan, focus and imagine, which can cause cognitive dissonance. The analytical mind can be cultivated and sharpened by engaging the mind.

Thinking is an activity of our biological nature; beyond this, little is known. Disturbed thoughts can be seen in brain wave patterns, and can be detected with an electroencephalographic test (ECG). Recently, the brain was found to possess an electromagnetic field. What do we mean by thinking? Thinking is everything the conscious mind does, including perception, mental arithmetic, memory, or manifesting an image. Thinking simply equates to a conscious cognition process. Psychoanalysis also can see what the unconscious is thinking.

Metaphorically speaking, the subconscious and synchronous conscious mind is like a garden. It is your responsibility to be aware of how this process works, but unfortunately for most of us, our role as a gardener has never been explained. We misunderstand this role; we have allowed seeds of all types, both good and bad, to enter the inner garden of our subconscious. Then, later we realize the weeds of bad or disturbing thoughts have grown out of proportion, and may become unmanageable. Consequently, our life becomes joyless because of such weeds.

In the science of thinking, we deal with how people acquire, process and store information. Thinking is an active process intimately connected with language. There is the active term thinking, while the passive term is a thought. We can call thought the product of the active process of thinking. Thought bubbles are usually full of words, with no pictures. Thus, spoken language is not necessary for thinking; thinking is inner speech.

So, who is in charge, you or your brain? The more you ask your brain to do, the more cortical space it sets up to handle new tasks. The evolution of man has caused the brain to become highly efficient at processing complex information, giving us a vast repertoire of possible thoughts. Our mind is our brain in action.

Thoughts are neither right nor wrong. They just are. It is what you want to do with your thoughts that introduces the rightness or wrongness. In other words, in the purported words of Martin Luther, "you cannot keep a bird from flying over your head; what you can do is prevent it from building a nest in your hair." Thus, it depends on what you do with your thoughts as to whether they are right or wrong.

We think we are our thoughts. This is the common core error in our shared human experience. You are not your thoughts. You are not even the observer of your thoughts. The thoughts that shape your personality came to you from parents, culture, religion, your social system, and so forth. Thus, you have to learn to regulate your mind; otherwise, it will menace you like the constant dripping of a leaky faucet.

Thought and behavior are intertwined. Since we talk about thought, it is worthwhile to talk briefly about behavior, because thoughts lead to behavior. What is behavior? Behavior is any observable activity of an animal, including humans. All the brain's building blocks are used to generate behavior. A person's behavior can be a response to a stimulus from our environment, but it can also be self-initiated behavior ranging from the simple, such as reflexes, to complex, such as talking. Behaviors can be instinctive or learned. Instinctive behavior is made up of rigid, stereotyped movement, while learned behaviors include any goal-directed behavior, like learning to play a sport or learning to drive.

As far as animals' behavior, those that live only a short time, such as insects, rely more on instinctive behaviors, while animals that live longer, like us, rely more on learned behaviors. We learn our behaviors from watching others, from instruction, and from trial and error. On any given day, our behavior is influenced by our genes and our environment, both physical and social. How we respond to a stimulus can be affected or modulated by our hormones, mood, attention level, health and personality. Our early life experiences can affect how we behaviorally respond to particular events later in life. These experiences can epigenetically modulate gene expression to stimuli years later. What are epigenetic mechanisms? They influence how genes act without changing the gene itself.

What happens to our mental ability when we grow older? It probably will be greater at 50 than it was at 20. In a study by the Office of Naval Research, 127 men who had taken the Army Alpha Examination when they entered Iowa State College after World War I were retested 30 years later. They were competing against their younger selves. The results showed they were intellectually more able at mean age 50 than they had been at mean age 19, when they were college freshmen.

The landscape of the human mind can be a complex of faculties involved in perceiving, remembering, considering, evaluating, and deciding, as well as such occurrences as sensation, emotions, memory, desires, various types of reasoning, motive, choices, personality traits, and the unconscious.

Chapter Two

The Nature of Thought

*The mind is the master power that molds and makes, and man is the mind;
evermore he takes the tool of thought, and shapes what he wills, bringing
forth a thousand joys, a thousand ills. He thinks in secret, and it comes to pass;
environment is but his looking-glass. – James Allen, <u>As a Man Thinketh</u>*

<u>The definition of thought</u>. The Oxford Dictionary defines thought as: the action or process of thinking, mental action or activity in general; especially that of intellect; the exercise of mental faculty; formation and arrangement of ideas in the mind.

Thoughts are the root cause of widespread sorrow and misery, which prevents humans from properly working together. This has its root in our ignorance of the general nature of the process of thought. Thoughts arise from the mind; it's possible the brain may merely serve as a notification device allowing us to become aware of thoughts put forth by the mind.

Thoughts come from the mind, and the mind comes from the brain. The mind is the brain in action. The brain is the mechanism behind creative thoughts; it is similar to having a pencil to draw a picture. The pencil is the brain, and the picture is the mind.

We live in a reality where we are shackled by our own intelligence, negative thoughts, and pride. We are prisoners of the brain inside our head. The formidable prison walls are fashioned of pride and arrogance and are very hard to breach. It is as if we worship the gateway, but are unable to take the leap of faith to step to the other side, to experience happiness. Thus happiness is elusive to us, because of our dominant thoughts that tend to oppose our happiness, and consider it not safe to our survival.

How do thoughts come to the mind, and how does thought work? Researcher Eric Leuthardt found that words are formed in the brain and find their way into the deepest recesses of the brain. Using electrodes, they found the area of the brain that is involved in creating the 40 or so sounds that form the English language. The brain generates a signal when people just think about the sounds, but it is very different from speaking. The implication is we can read people's private thoughts as well as what they want to say.

Do you own the thoughts that occur to you?, asks Keith Rayne, in his book *Life in Autopilot*. At the ordinary moment when something occurs to you, do you wonder where it comes from? There are "orphan thoughts", especially common when we encounter someone different from us. Some people see a Pakistani in an airport and think "suicide bomber." Others see a young black on the street and think, "mugger", so there is an outside stimulus which forces us to develop certain thoughts.

This is why we say we are the reflection of our outside world; 90% of our thoughts are a copy of another day or month or year. Originality is less than 5% of our thoughts. Others put in us their thoughts and we tend to buy into it. For example, stereotypical thoughts like those above cross our mind consciously, even though we do not agree with them. Where do these come from? They are uninvited thoughts, which simply show up, like a cognitive spasm, without control over them.

We have always assumed that thoughts originate in the brain. It seems this assumption is not correct. Our thoughts originate from outside our bodies. The brain does not create our thoughts, but rather processes them and tries to adapt them to our ability to understand and function.

As creative tools, we can look at the mind and body like a radio. The structure of our body is like an antenna. It is especially designed for sensing and amplifying a particular type of energy, and ultimately determines our receptiveness to the energy of creation. Because of our body, the energy we sense tends to hold our awareness localized in physical experiences, as with a radio. There may be some stray signals and noise, but in general the "radio" will be concentrated on the "signal" we select by tuning our radio, and we will hear a particular broadcast.

We understand that our desires or plans are the result of electro-chemical processes taking place in our brain, but what triggers these activities? Is it the brain itself? The answer is no. Thoughts enter our brain from sources outside of our physical body, and only when they reach the brain does it begin to act and decipher them. However, the human mind has a reservoir of experiences that normally is stored in the subconscious mind. When we see events which remind us of a past event, then we experience the worry and good or bad events we experienced before

Anil K. Rajvanshi, in 2004, said that no matter what we draw from life's thinking, good or bad, high or low, heated or cool, thoughts are emotional or stoical, intelligent or stupid, concentrated or scattered. The mind is the name given to the sum of the states of consciousness, grouped under thoughts, will, and feeling. Just as the process of digestion relates to the stomach, the process of thinking relates to the brain. There is no problem more important, or more daunting than discovering the structure and process behind human thought. J. Krishnamurti, in *What is Thought* says thought is a material process; a process performed by biochemical reactions in the brain cells.

There are three types of thoughts:

1. <u>Pathological thought</u>. Pathological thinking does not see itself; when it does, it dissolves like a witch in water, mixed with emotion and unrecognizable. Pathological thoughts A) Have emotion; B) Do not see themselves; C) Do not see other types of thought; D) Are imbalanced by emotion; and E) Are disturbed by anger and jealousy.

The purpose of pathological thought is to justify and express emotion. The purpose is not to think, but to use thought as a means to an end. It is not designed for logic. Pathological thought also steals energy from the sex center in the brain and leads to a variety of personal and social difficulties.

2. <u>Logical thought</u>. Logical thought can see only itself, is not common, and requires some attention to the steps of thinking. This type of thinking requires some training, and some intelligence. People know how they differentiate among several factors. Often though, people are not logical and go against their logic. But such self-defeating behavior is embedded in the unconscious mind. Thus, logical thinking can be a rarity when it comes to human transactions.

3. <u>Psychological thought</u>. These are always seen, along with other thoughts. Psychological thinking is self-evaluating. It is processed by reflection; it has

understanding and goals. For example: "I wish to understand why I am upset with Lela," is a thought conscious of itself.

In the 20th century, the philosophy of the mind became one of the central areas of philosophy in the English-speaking world, and remains so, with questions regarding the relationship between the mind and the brain. The nature of consciousness, and how we perceive the world, has come to be seen as crucial in understanding the world. The aims are to understand mental phenomena regarding the operation of the mind; this subject is called cognitive science.

Rene Descartes (1596-1650) saw that all humans consist of materials subject to the normal laws of physics, and the immaterial mind, which is not. This dual nature gives Descartes' theory its name: Cartesian Dualism. The immaterial mind causes the actions of the body. Through the brain, perceptions are fed to the mind from the body. Descartes thought this interaction between mind and body took place in the part of the brain we call the pineal gland. However, his concept was challenged by behaviorist and psychologist B.F. Skinner's claims that mental events can be reduced to stimulus response pairs.

Chapter Three

The Mysteries of the Mind

*There is no scientific study more vital to man then the study
of his own mind. The mind is its own place, and in itself
can make a heaven of hell, a hell of heaven. – Allen
Our life is what our thoughts make it. – Marcus Aurelius.*

If you try to force the mind to travel in a certain direction, it will go the other way. That is one of the greatest mysteries of the mind. If you keep thinking about something you do not want, you will get exactly that thing. This is the real mystery of the mind.

The problem cannot be solved at the same level of awareness that created it; you must have another level of awareness to solve it. The world we have created is a process of our thinking; it cannot be changed without changing our thinking. The intuitive mind is a sacred gift and the rational mind is a faithful servant. We have created a society that honors the servant and has forgotten the gift (Einstein).

Our power as humans derives from our ability to think, to articulate, and translate thoughts into action. Our power is unmatched by any other species on earth. After all, we are the most adaptable species.

The Sanskrit word for "mind", *Dukkha*, means container or dissatisfaction. As they say, "it is easier to tame a thousand horses then to tame the mind." Buddha indicated the mind is not an obedient servant, it has a mind of its own. In the same vein Buddha also said all our problems are caused by the instilled mind. These are the painful facts about the mind, and once we understand this dynamic, we learn to deal with the mind effectively. Otherwise, we may never be able to deal with the sly mind.

9

Have you ever taken a course on how to manage the mind, or ever read a book on how to think? Schools do not teach people how to think, nor do parents teach us how to figure out the answers. Thus, it is mandatory to teach the science of the mind. School systems all over the world need to teach children how they can manage their thinking, and how to use the faculty of reasoning. Reasoning is crucial to avert serious mental health problems. It can be the best investment the human community can make, because the result is people who know how to manage their thoughts.

It is fascinating to see a flood of magazines trumpeting the latest theories about how to be physically fit, and how to lose weight, but we do not see any magazine articles about how to sharpen the thinking process, how to enhance thinking skills, or enrich mind management skills. However, it is not what you think, but how you think it, because thinking has a huge effect on how your place in the world. Much of what we do not understand about being human is in our heads. The brain is a befuddling organ, as are the questions of life and death, consciousness, sleep and much more.

The mind is a brain in action; an entity which has the nature of experiences, defined by clarity and knowing. Within the mind are gross levels, such as sensory perceptions, which cannot function or even come into being without a physical organism like our senses. Mental consciousness is heavily dependent upon physiological factors.

Another distinctive feature of the mind is its capacity to observe and examine itself. For instance, examining past experiences, you recall experiences and examine memories. Thus, when we talk about the mind, we talk about a highly intricate network of different mental events and states of self-consciousness, or self-awareness.

If you want a new life, then you have to have a new mind; in order to change external conditions, you must first change internal conditions. Unfortunately, most people omit this step. They try to change external conditions by working directly on those conditions. That always proves futile, or at best temporary, unless it is accompanied by a change of thoughts and beliefs.

Sir Swami Savanna talked about the mystery of the mind, and characterized it with the following:

1) The mind is not only made daily, but hourly. In every minute it changes color and shape like a chameleon.

2) The mind has a pernicious nature of externalization.

3) The mind can send only one kind of sensation at a time for the manufacture of a perception or concept.

4) Secretions from endocrine glands – the Thyroid, Thymus, Parotid, Pineal, and Suprarenal – are directly absorbed into the blood. They play a vital part in constituting the temperament of every individual. The temperament of an individual can be greatly modified by environment, education and experiences.

5) To understand the subtlety of the mind is to understand the havoc of imagination. Imaginary fears of various sorts, concoctions, mental dramatizations, or building castles in the air, are all clues to the power of imagination. Even a perfectly healthy person has some imaginary disease or other due to the power of the imagination. Much energy is wasted on imaginary fears.

6) Belief, reasoning, and faith are all tools to understand what is around you, but the mind tends to get carried away with belief, and develops self-righteousness.

7) The mind always wants to attach to an object to cherish, and feels happy in this attachment. It is difficult to divert the mind that has fallen into the pernicious habit of seeking pleasure outwardly.

8) In the vast majority the mind has been allowed to run wild and follow its own will and desires. It is like a spoiled child or badly trained dog. Restraining the mind is unknown to most persons.

9) The mind visualizes any object it intently focuses on. For example, if you think of an orange, then the mind sees an orange. If you think of a king riding an elephant, that's what the mind sees. Thus, you must train the mind properly with a healthy mental image.

10) The mind is ever changing and wandering, this wandering habit manifests itself in various ways, and we have to be alert always to keep this wandering in check. It is similar to a monkey, because a monkey never stays on one tree; rather, it jumps from one to another. The wandering must be controlled, or otherwise we suffer. Teach the mind one thing at a time.

11) If all thoughts are eliminated, there remains nothing which can be called the mind. Thoughts are the mind. There is no such thing as a

world independent of and apart from thoughts. Thought is central to our existence.

The law of attraction. There is a universal law of attraction and polarity, pitting your mind against your unconscious negative beliefs. You are inadvertently setting yourself up to attract more of the same unwanted circumstances through the law of attraction and polarity. Like attracts like, which means the private conversation you have within yourself attracts energy to be manifested. For example, if you decide to lose weight, then the mind works against that, because the mind attracts the unwanted behavior. Instead, decide to have a healthy lifestyle. Everything is energy, and whatever you put out there, it tends to come to you. This is why we try to set the mind upon the things we want to happen, not that which we do not want.

The trouble with most of us is we tend to focus on what we do not want. We put energy into that, and the brain follows the energy where we are putting it. The brain does not realize this is what we want. With the law of attraction, you put energy and attention on what you want or hope for, and your mind will attract that. For example, if you want to have wealth, or a great partner, focus the energy there and the universe will bring it to you.

Our thoughts are very powerful and tend to bring to us what we hope for, not the opposite. There is subtlety in how you formulate your intentions and energy on what you want, and not on what you don't. You need to be clear in what you want, so when you send the message to the universe, it is accurate. Returning to the weight problem example, you may send the message that you do not like your body; thus, the weight stays with you, since your energy is focused on what you dislike. Instead send the message that you would like to have a healthy lifestyle. The energy will be focused then on health, and eventually the weight will disappear.

The concept of the monkey came from Buddha, and says our mind tends to wander most of the time, like a monkey who jumps from tree to tree. The mind wanders aimlessly, never staying still; this is a source of our disturbance. Because the mind takes us to unwanted places and experiences, it can make life a living hell. Our mind is an enemy, not our friend. Thus, we have to guard ourselves from the intruder that keeps hunting for problems without mercy.

Our mind is not built to make us happy; it is built to help us survive. So far, it has done a great job. But in the process, it developed some bad habits, like avoiding new experiences or scrounging for problems where none exist. No wonder that worry, bad moods, and self-critical thoughts so often get in the way of enjoying life. Shawn Smith, from his book *The Human Mind*, said, "The mind is always looking out for us, even when it seems to be working against us." That is a lesson learned through thousands of generations of expert survivors. The problem is, the mind often tries to save our lives, even when our lives are not really at stake. Thus, as the old bumper-sticker goes. "do not believe everything you think."

The mind works like a nervous dog in the backyard, barking frantically at every passing squirrel, or smelling a human from a far distance, even though that human never constitutes any danger to the dog. Over time, dogs allowed to continue with such behavior become louder, more frantic, and more aggressive. As annoying and irrational as it may seem to others, the dog's behavior makes sense from the dog's perspective.

This is exactly what is happening to the mind. It tends to detect a presumed danger from a great distance. In reality, there is no danger, but we cannot argue with the mind, because it will outmaneuver us by any means. If we ask the mind to think of an object, it seems to obey us for a moment, but soon it takes its own course, wandering off. If you ask your mouth to keep shut, it obeys you, if you shut your eyes, they will obey you. But if you ask your mind not to think, it will do the opposite, because the mind keeps blabbering inwardly, and most thinking is done in an automatic manner. If you let your mind behave as it likes and give it complete freedom, you will lose your freedom completely. Moreover, reality is the product of the mind, and if you can change the way you think, you can change your reality.

The mind is a pattern recognition system; it creates, stores, and recognizes patterns. The mind can and does create and stores its own patterns, and later recognizes them when presented with data. Thinking involves the reproduction of previously learned responses and associations. It can fathom the beginning of time, and the end of the universe. However, the mind isn't capable of understanding itself, with billions of neurons, which makes the mind a tough nut to crack.

Every animal you can think of -- mammals, birds, reptiles, fish, and amphibians -- has a brain, but the human brain is unique. It is not the largest, but it gives us power, and is truly an amazing and fascinating organ. As Plutarch put it, "the mind is not a vessel to be filled, but a fire to be kindled."

The brain performs an incredible number of tasks including blood pressure, heart rate and breathing.

The mind accepts a flood of information about the world around us from our various senses: seeing, hearing, smelling, tasting and touching; it lets you think, dream, reason and experience emotions. The brain makes up only 2 % of our body weight, but it uses 20% of the energy we consume. Neurons keep changing throughout life; they continue to form new connections, strengthen existing connections, or eliminate connections as we continue to learn. This is called brain plasticity. (There is a chapter in the book about this.)

While the brain has physical characteristics which can be visualized, touched, handled and located inside of the skull, the mind has no physical dimension. But there is a relationship between them. For example when the brain is blocked by deep anesthesia or coma, the mind also does not seem to function. The mind is not gross matter (visible or tangible); it cannot be seen. Magnitudes of the mind cannot be measured; it does not require a space to exist. The mind is nothing but a bundle of desires, thoughts, wants, and expectations, and all those functions are continually changing. For example, we have a lot of ambitions and dreams logged into our mind since childhood, and we carry them around throughout our lives.

Types of thinking. Convergent thinking focuses on a single problem and suitable solution. Divergent thinking focuses on many possibilities, brainstorming and gathering from all sources. Edison indicated that 5 percent of people think, 10 percent of people think they think, and the other 85 percent would rather die than think. But thinking is a skill, and we need to learn it. Unfortunately, most people do not know how to think; it can be hard, because it requires attention, concentration, and focus, as well as detachment from previous experiences.

The conscious mind consists of all the mental processes of which we are aware. If you feel thirsty, you get a drink; it is logic and reasoning ability. Any operation in our daily life must go through the conscious mind, and then it will be referred to the unconscious mind. Normally the conscious mind cannot tolerate painful experiences and just refers them to the unconscious mind.

The <u>unconscious mind</u> contains biological instincts (Eros and Thanatos), sexual urges, and aggression. It contains all sorts of disturbing materials we need to keep out of our awareness. They constitute serious threats to our ego and are unacceptable or unpleasant, such as feelings of pain, anxiety or psychic conflict, and tend to influence our behavior without our awareness. It is like a Trojan horse. The unconscious mind is a reservoir of feelings, thoughts and memories which are out of our consciousness and we tend to forget or suppress them. They are powerful and very potent, and may direct behavior without our awareness.

The <u>collective unconscious</u>. Carl Jung came up with the very sophisticated concept that we all have collective experiences that are stored in each particular species. They are not developed individually, but, are inherited from our ancestors. These innate thoughts have shaped the mind, like fear of snakes, or the response to sudden noises.

<u>Conscious vs. unconscious thinking</u>. When you try to change a habit, you find your unconscious mind is resisting. A basic law of the nature of the mind is, whenever your conscious and unconscious are in conflict, invariably your unconscious wins. Whenever imagination and logic are in conflict, imagination usually wins. For example, a dieter thinks logically to reduce weight, while imagination reminds them of the good taste of food. Eventually the imagination tends to win and they keep eating. Thus, the diet doesn't work. Your unconscious mind is like autopilot, while your conscious mind is manual control.

The mind is like spring water; it cannot flow salty and fresh at the same time. Opposing ideas cannot be held at the same time. For example, negative and positive thoughts cannot be in the mind at the same time.

<u>Seeing and hearing</u>. Often we only see what we believe in our mind, not what we actually see. The mind has a filter which injects stored materials, (wishes and desires) and lets you see them. We also do not hear what we actually hear; we hear what pleases our unconscious wishes and desires. Thus, we may think reality is in our mind, but it's not the actual reality. This is one of the human dilemmas that makes us biased by nature.

The conditioning and the stored materials in our mind tend to distract us, and often make our lives painful. Thus, psychology constantly attempts to correct our perceptions, and prove to us that reality is not what we think, but is totally different. In psychotherapy we try to guide the patient to decipher what is real and not real, as well as putting a cap on the individual catastrophic imaginings that contaminate our lives.

Chapter Four

Our Conscious and Unconscious Mind

When we wake up in the morning, we perceive that the sun is rising, hear birds chirping and feel the fresh morning air as it hits our face. In other words, we are conscious. The neuroscientists are serious about this topic; the greatest brain teaser in the field is how the brain gives rise to subjective experiences. There are, however, numerous questions we still have no answer.

The University of Pennsylvania researched oxygen consumption in a group of subjects while they idled, did a problem, or slept. They found virtually no change throughout. The conclusion: your brain uses most of its energy merely in keeping circuits alive and sensitive, and needs little more when you use the circuits. So the brain uses more energy preparing to solve a problem, not when solving it. The peak of body temperature and mental acuity occurs in the middle of the working period. We think faster than we speak; we speak an average of 125-169 words per minute, while thinking is four times faster. When we think, we are basically talking to ourselves.

It is almost a truism that we are our own worst enemies when it comes to understanding ourselves and thinking clearly. How can we explore the less accessible parts of our mind and personality, to enable us to think more clearly and make decisions more in tune with our whole personality, rather than purely rational factors?

Thoughts are generated by the mind. All behavior results from the thoughts that preceded it. So the thing to work on is not behavior, but the thing that caused it, which is your thought (Wayne Dyer).

David Hume defines consciousness as the activities of our five senses and the processing of them by our brain. However, during sleep our five senses are put to sleep, in a way, and our brain recreates the stimulation of our senses from our memories, to depict needs, wants, and beliefs through our dreams.

The analogy of the human mind and the computer is often made, one of many possible metaphors and the most commonly used. The mind is a super computer-greater, better and more efficient than any computer. Just as any computer can run many different programs, the brain can perform many different behaviors, as well. Both the computer and the human mind store files and programs in memory until they are needed. Thus, the unconscious mind stores incredible volumes of experiences and memories, and we access them when we face similar experiences. Often, the unconscious mind stores negative experiences.

Brain researchers are puzzled by consciousness. For example, if you look at a painting, you are aware of shape and color, but at the same time the visual impression could stir up emotions and thoughts inside of you. This subjective awareness and perception is consciousness, and is the delineation between humans and other animals. Why does awareness exist in the first place, or what truly is it to be human? Once we fully understand and unravel the mysteries of human consciousness, the mysteries of our cognitive universe unfold.

Metaphorically, the subconscious mind is like a super computer, compared to your conscious mind, which is a laptop. The subconscious mind is more than 80 times more powerful than the conscious mind. Thoughts pop into your head without our permission, and that makes the unconscious mind the source of our disturbance.

Psychoanalyst Sigmund Freud believed behavior and personality derive from the constant and unique interaction of conflicting psychological forces that operate at three levels of awareness: the preconscious, the conscious, and the unconscious. The unconscious includes thoughts, emotions, memories, desires and motivations outside of our awareness, yet continues to exert an influence on our behavior.

The conscious mind includes everything of which we are aware. This is the aspect of mental processing which we can think and talk about rationally. A part of this includes memory, which is not always part of consciousness, but can be retrieved easily at any time and brought into awareness. The conscious mind is responsible for logic and reasoning. If you are asked the sum of three plus three, it is your conscious mind that is going to be used for that calculation. It also controls all intended actions while conscious. For example, if you want to move your hand, the conscious mind does it. It is a gatekeeper for the mind.

It works like a filter. For example, if someone calls you stupid, the conscious mind realizes the statement.

The preconscious mind represents ordinary memory. While we are not aware of this information at any given time, we can retrieve it and pull it into consciousness when needed. That is why affirmations make no sense and can never improve our beliefs, because affirmations are on the conscious level and are always filtered by the subconscious mind, because they usually do not match your belief system.

The unconscious mind is a reservoir of feelings, thoughts, urges, and memories outside of conscious awareness. Most of the contents of the unconscious are unacceptable or unpleasant, such as feelings of pain, anxiety, or conflict. According to Freud, the unconscious continues to influence our behavior, and experiences, even though we are unaware of these underlying influences.

Freud likened these three levels of mind to an iceberg. The top of the iceberg you can see above water represents the conscious mind. The part of the iceberg that is submerged below water but is still visible is the preconscious. The bulk of the iceberg unseen beneath the waterline represents the unconscious, and is huge. The subconscious mind is responsible for all involuntary actions. Breathing, heart rate, and emotions are controlled by the unconscious mind, and it is also where beliefs and memory are stored.

How do the conscious and unconscious mind work? Think of the unconscious mind as the storage room of everything that is currently not in your conscious mind. The unconscious mind stores all of your previous life experiences. As to how they work together, think of a person learning to drive. At the beginning, the person is focused on the dashboard, steering, and is nervous, because he is still using the conscious mind to drive. A few weeks later, driving becomes a habit that happens automatically without needing to think about it. Now you can use your cell phone, or hold a conversation while you drive. Because this specific skill has been transferred to the unconscious mind, the conscious mind is operating it no longer.

Living forever may not be a reality, but pioneers in a field called Cryonics may give people second lives. Cryonic centers, like the Alcore Life Extension Foundation of Arizona, store human bodies in vats filled with liquid nitrogen at temperatures of minus 320 degrees Fahrenheit (195 Celsius). The idea is a person who dies from a presently incurable disease could be thawed and revived in the future when a cure has been found. The body of late baseball legend Ted

Williams is stored in one of Alcor's freezers, but the cure does not yet exist. In cryonics, both the conscious and unconscious mind are lost.

We can examine the human mind and see how these three levels work together and create reality. Freud made these terms popular in mainstream society. The conscious mind occupies not more than 10% of the mind; below that is a large slice of the pie, the preconscious, sometimes called subconscious. The unconscious mind occupies the whole width of the base of the triangle and fills out the other 30-40%. It is vast and deep and largely inaccessible to conscious thoughts, like the dark depths of the ocean.

The conscious mind is what most people associate with who you are, because most people live day to day. But it is by no means where all the action takes place. The conscious mind communicates to the outside world through speech, pictures, writing, physical movement, and thoughts. The subconscious mind is in charge of recent memories, and is in continuous contact with the resources of the unconscious mind.

The unconscious mind is the storehouse of all memories and past experiences. These memories have been repressed through trauma, and have simply been consciously forgotten, and are no longer important to us. It is from these memories and experiences that our beliefs, habits and behavior are formulated. Moreover, the unconscious mind, via our subconscious, gives us meaning to interact with the world as filtered through feelings, emotion, imagination, sensation, and dreams.

The unconscious mind is similar to the subconscious mind in that both deal with memories, but there are differences between the two. The unconscious mind is the cellar, the underground library of all memories, habits, and behavior. It is the storehouse of all deep seated emotion that has been programmed since birth. Any real change in our behavior should address this part of the mind.

So what is the difference between the subconscious and the unconscious? "Unconscious" is a term used by psychologists and psychiatrists regarding thoughts we have which are out of reach of the conscious. It is the storage place for all memories that have been repressed and do not wish to recall, such as traumatic childhood events which have been blocked out, or certain memories that are very hard to retrieve. The subconscious, on the other hand, is almost the same, but the major difference is we can choose to remember. Because it is closer to the surface, it is easily accessible with a little focus. For example, if I ask about a phone number, you are not conscious of it, but can bring it from the subconscious easily, because it is in the "RAM" of this computer. The role of the unconscious is perhaps the same as the subconscious, but the unconscious is the source of everything in the subconscious.

How can you change your life? You have to change the core level of your "program", held in your unconscious mind. You may use visualization to influence the program in the subconscious mind, which is constantly running. If you put enough emotional energy and focus on your conscious thinking, you will start to reprogram your internal beliefs and perceptions. When that happens, you will experience change on a very deep level. It is a top down approach. After all, that is how your habits, behavior, and beliefs were created in the first place.

Freud compared himself to an archaeologist, digging away layers of the human mind, and identified three separate areas of the mind. He described the conscious mind, which consists of all the mental processes of which we are aware. The unconscious mind contains biological based instincts (Eros and Thanatos), the primitive urges for sex, and aggression. It contains very important materials which are kept buried; nevertheless, they exert a significant influence.

He also identified the psyche with three levels as well: the Id, which is unconscious, and the Ego and Superego, which are conscious. We grow in our psyche either flowers or weeds in the garden of our life. Whichever, we plant by the mental equivalents we create. The conscious mind determines the action, the unconscious mind determines the reaction, and the reaction is just as important as the action.

The unconscious mind's first and foremost purpose is to preserve the body; it will fight anything that appears to be a threat to survival. Thus, if you want to change a behavior more easily, show your unconscious how this behavior is hurting you. It's also the unconscious which runs the body, and handles all of your basic physical functions, like breathing, heart rate, and the immune system. It is also like a child, in that it wants a clear direction, it takes your instruction very literally. So if you say for example, "this job is a pain in the neck", your unconscious will figure out a way to make sure that your neck is hurting you at work.

Whatever you put in the unconscious, it tends to stay. It tends to communicate through emotion and symbols. To get your attention, it uses emotions. For example, if you suddenly feel afraid, your unconscious has detected, (rightly or wrongly), that your survival is at risk. Moreover, it tends to exaggerate the risk. Even if there is no risk, it tends to give you the feeling that you are in deep trouble.

The unconscious decides where, when, and how memories are stored. It may hide certain memories, such as trauma, with which you may have strong negative emotions until you are mature enough to process them consciously. It brings other memories to you so you can deal with them. It also makes associations and learns quickly, to protect you. The unconscious stays alert and tries to glean the lesson from each experience. For example, if you had bad experiences in school, the unconscious tends to lump all of your learning experiences into bad feelings, resulting in sweaty palms and anxiety whenever you attempt something new.

Let us follow the computer analogy to clarify how these three concepts work. Imagine your mind is like a computer; your conscious mind is best represented by the keyboard and monitor. Data is input on the keyboard and the results are on the monitor screen. This is how the conscious mind works. Information is taken in via external or internal stimuli, and the results are instantaneously put into the consciousness. The subconscious is the RAM -- Random Access Memory -- in your computer. Any recent memories are stored, like programs you run every day, such as thought patterns, habits and feelings.

The unconscious mind is the hard disk drive; it is long term storage for all memories and programs that have been installed since birth, and the data that you receive from the world to keep you safe and ensure your survival. The logic of these two, subconscious and unconscious, look in the past to help you manage similar situations, even if painful, and exaggerate the difficulties.

Often the unconscious mind does not obey the commands of the conscious mind. For example, if you are lying in bed at night and hear some noise in the house, the unconscious mind starts to imagine something wrong might happen. Then your subconscious will send feelings, emotions, and memories of past events that are associated with those thoughts. The subconscious wants to protect you and prepare you to face the situation.

Our thoughts are probably the only true freedom we have in this world, as we can actually control them. A man can be physically trapped in prison with inhuman conditions, and yet still be free in his mind. Victor Franklin and Nelson Mandela are testament to that. We alone can choose how we are going to respond to our experiences in life, requiring serious mental toughness.

The other ability of the conscious mind is the ability to use the imagination to create something which may not exist, while your unconscious mind can only offer versions of the stored memories of your past experiences. However, the unconscious mind does not differentiate between what the conscious mind creates, or the real thing, and it tends to recall emotions and feelings associated with that image.

For example if you dream about winning Lotto, or meeting with someone special, then the unconscious supplies you with joyful feelings as if this actually happened to you. But often, the unconscious mind does not intend to bring joyful events to the surface, but rather brings the painful memories and attaches false feelings to them. That is the nature of the sly mind. It refuses to be controlled. This is the whole theme of the book.

The power of conscious imagination has been tested using three groups practicing baseball. One group practiced and improved 24% of the time. The second group did not practice and understandably did not improve. But the third group imagined practicing for twenty minutes a day, and they improved 23%, almost the same as the group actually practicing. Thus, never underestimate the power of visualization of the conscious mind. It can change your life for better or for worse. It depends on the way you use it.

It is not easy to change what has been stored in the unconscious, because the default programs have too much energy attached to them to change, unless pain is associated with them. Then a major shift may take place. Otherwise, the old program will reemerge.

The mandate of the subconscious is to attract circumstances and situations that match the images you have within. Let us use the analogy that your subconscious mind is like deep fertile soil that accepts any seeds you plant within in. Your habitual thoughts and beliefs are the seeds that are constantly sown, and in your life, they produce what is sown. As surely as corn kernels produce corn and wheat seeds produce wheat, your thoughts will have an effect on your life. You will reap what you sow. The conscious mind is the gardener. It is its responsibility to be aware of how this process works and to wisely choose what reaches the garden.

Unfortunately for most of us, our role as gardener has never been explained to us. We misunderstand this role; we have allowed seeds of all types, both good and bad, to enter the inner garden of the unconscious mind. The unconscious mind will not discriminate, judge or censor. It will manifest success, abundance and health, just as easily as failure, ill health, and misfortune. It works to reproduce in our life what seeds have been nurtured within. Your subconscious accepts what is impressed upon it with feelings and repetition, whether those thoughts are positive or negative. It does not evaluate things like your conscious mind does.

Once we understand that our unconscious will bring whatever we need, want, or desire, and then project the thoughts and images of what you want, seemingly chance and fortuitous events will begin to happen. This powerful inner collaborator, working with your conscious mind, will bring to you people and circumstances which allow you to achieve your goals. A thousand unseen hands, as Joseph Campbell described them, will come to your aid. Synchronicity appears, to the uninitiated, to be coincidence or luck, but it is neither. It is simply the operation of natural laws which you have set in motion with your thoughts.

Modern physics now sees the universe as a vast inseparable web of dynamic activities. Not only is the universe alive and constantly changing, but everything in the universe affects everything else. At its most primary level, the universe seems to be whole and undifferentiated, a fathomless sea of energy that permeates every object and every act, because we all are a parts of one giant universe of dynamic energy.

Everything in the universe is made up of energy. The chair that you are sitting on is comprised of energy. The walls of the room that you are now in, your computer, the events that happen to you are all made by the liberation of energy. Our thoughts too, are vibrations of energy. Our thoughts are of the exact same substances as the building blocks of the universe. Once we become aware of this remarkable fact, we can use it to our great advantage. Thus, we have to train our thoughts to attract the best into our lives, and avoid attracting the bad. Sadly, the latter is the predominating force in our lives. Overall though, we have the ability to change and live a joyful and meaningful life.

Chapter Five

The Power of the Unconscious Mind

Most of us are aware that we have something called an unconscious mind within us, but we know very little about it, let alone how to harness it. We need to learn to make the unconscious mind an ally in achieving success in life. You need to establish a working relationship with the unconscious mind. To do this, one must become conscious of and familiar with this hidden, mysterious aspect of us and the role it plays in life.

One of the ways to do this is by affirming, for several minutes each day, that our unconscious is our partner in success. We are educating ourselves that we possess a second powerful mind, and it is our partner in success. Becoming conscious of our unconscious and moving beyond what resides in it, is an abstract concept, a figment of imagination, but it is an important step by itself. The next step is to be aware of how our conscious and unconscious are working together, and to learn the function and roles of each.

The unconscious has two main functions in life. The first is to attract the conditions and circumstances according to the predominant thought patterns that reside within it; what you focus on, you attract. With this new unconscious information, you can begin to understand why this is true. Your unconscious mind is not limited in any way, and will forever attract according to your thoughts. It has no volition of its own, and will simply act upon what resides and vibrates within you.

The mind becomes the source of our misery, because the unconscious mind and even the conscious mind become the garbage bin of society; they bring the trash to you, and you accept it, and it becomes part of your psychological makeup. There is no inner engineering to your unconscious mind; you just let it be, and that can have serious consequences for you and your quality of life.

However, your unconscious mind will act upon any request or instruction you give it. Any thought that is repeated over and over again will imprint within the unconscious mind, because it cannot distinguish between what is real and what is imagined. This is why visualization, affirmation and repeated images can have powerful effects. By doing these exercises we are creating an image within ourselves which the unconscious then acts upon.

Our conscious mind is the guardian to the gates of the unconscious. It is the conscious mind's role to make sure only the highest quality thoughts gain entrance to the unconscious. When we fully understand how whatever thoughts and beliefs gain entrance to the unconscious will eventually manifest in life, we become very diligent in monitoring and directing our thoughts carefully.

The conscious mind has limited memory, most of it short term. The unconscious mind, in stark contrast, has a virtually infinite memory. You are probably thinking it does not seem that way to you; you have enough memory for everything you have experienced in your life. It is your recall that is fallible. Moreover, when your unconscious mind and conscious are in conflict, your unconscious wins, but only if you do not know how to control it. Your unconscious mind is the genie and it is the master, while the conscious mind stimulates the unconscious into actions like changing habits, reversing negative thinking patterns, or improving physical and emotional health. Our unconscious can even influence involuntary function, like heart rate, breathing, or blood pressure.

The following chart sums up the differences between the conscious and unconscious mind:

Characteristic	Conscious Mind	Unconscious Mind
Age	new	old
Size	small	large
Sight	sees	blind
Communication through	feelings	images
Cognitive Process	logical	illogical
Majority of thoughts	mature	immature
Time	past, present, future	present

Characteristic	Conscious Mind	Unconscious Mind
Will power	will	power
Functions	voluntary	involuntary
Functions at one time	one	trillions
Memory	limited	unlimited
Control	master of the unconscious	body and behavior

Willpower. The conscious mind has the sense of awareness. It knows persons, places, conditions, and thinking. It has the ability to initiate and direct thought or action. However, the brain is a source of electrical energy; it can do electrical work, and your brain produces about 25 watts of power. The unconscious mind transmits this energy as urges, emotions, impulses, nervous twitches, etc. The energy in the unconscious mind is inexhaustible. Thus, your brain functions 24 hours a day all of your life.

Using the conscious mind requires tremendous effort, just as learning something for the first time takes effort. For example, it took a while to learn to tie a shoestring, but once you learned it became a habit, relegated to the unconscious. It's now an easy habit you do not have to think about; it became unconscious. Thus, the conscious mind has the will to do things, and the unconscious mind has the power.

Emile Coue (1857-1926) was highly successful in Europe curing a variety of illnesses, by using an affirmation (everyday, better and better in every way), as well as the power of suggestion. He said, "when will and imagination are in conflict, imagination always wins." That is to say, when the conscious and the unconscious mind are in conflict, the unconscious always wins, because it has the power, both electrical and chemical.

When an overweight person has the will to go on a diet, and does not change the unconscious desire for overeating, eventually the unconscious mind will win out. That person will gain back any weight lost. You can will yourself not to eat that delicious dessert, but the urge from the unconscious mind will win. You will eat the dessert and do so effortlessly. Our task is to learn how the unconscious mind works and use it to our advantage, because although it has the power to determine, it is not as smart as your conscious mind.

Underlining the power of our unconscious mind. Neuroscience has proven that our unconscious mind is eager to serve us, in any way that we need, and is serving you right now in the following: A) Processing the 11 million bits of information you receive every day; B) Driving nearly 95% of the decisions you make and the actions you take; C) Running every system and cell in your body. We are the cause of our unconscious mind. When we are thoughtful in our communication with ourselves and others, we guide our unconscious mind in a positive way. When we get stuck repeating negative thoughts and behavior, we direct our unconscious mind in limited directions.

Is it really that simple? Yes, if you: A) Focus on what you want. Our unconscious mind does not process negative or positive. For example, when I say, do not think about your competitors, you think about them, do you not? When we focus on an unwanted thing, that will happen. The first shift to clearly direct your unconscious mind is to focus on the positive thing that you want. Concentrate on what you want in your thoughts, your communication with others, or in the events that take place in your life.

B) Pause to find objectivity. Our unconscious mind is designed to take everything personally. Our personal perception forms our reality. We apply our inner perception to the world, or project our truth to explain everything that occurs in our space. Unfortunately, our perceptions and projections often stray far from reality, and they may come from the recesses of our unconscious mind.

The second step to finding your objectivity, is to practice jumping in front of a knee-jerk response that personalizes life's experiences, and deprives you of not being clear or objective in your responses. For example when you flare at an email, before you hit reply, pause, take a breath and stop the program your unconscious mind is running. Step into alternative realities of the situation, and brainstorm what other options the sender might by trying to communicate to you.

C) Feed objective reality back into your unconscious mind. You can upgrade the personalizing programs and evolve to a more objective perception. D) Success is in repetition. Just as we learn a new sport or language, we create behavior and thinking habits by repetition. Repetition is the mother of learning. We must be consistent as we replace old patterns with fresh perceptions.

Simply shifting our thoughts for a day or week is not enough to change unconscious habits and thoughts; change may develop over time. This shift chases the change you want to make and sticks with it. Repeat positive thoughts, return to objectivity and stay consistent, and most unconscious programming can and will shift within 30 days with focus, determination and repetition.

Earl Nightingale said "whatever we plant in our unconscious mind and nourish with repetition and emotion will one day become a reality." It is a storeroom with limited capacity; all memories, past experiences, deepest beliefs, everything that has ever happened to you is permanently stored. In simple terms, the unconscious is a part of you outside of your conscious awareness. It creates automatic programs to make functioning in life easier, without having to pay attention to everything you are doing.

Your unconscious mind is the master program for your life, consistent with your self-concept. That is why it is important for you to filter what is embedded there. Your thoughts have the power to manifest in reality; the choice is yours. you are aware. Albert Einstein said, "We cannot solve our problems with the same thinking we used to create them." Thus, we need a different level of thinking to solve problems. We see people fail to solve problems, because they use the same frame of mind that created them. We have to create a new understanding and fresh perspectives to solve our problems.

In breaking down established neural pathways to change our lives, we need to do more than change thoughts; we have to go deeper and change our programming. To reprogram the unconscious mind with the present conscious understanding you have gained, takes tremendous time and energy. It involves creating new neural connections in your brain. In spite of negative patterns or bad habits, you can do it, by spending time each day affirming new beliefs or thoughts. By affirming a new thought pattern, you can effectively change your life and reality.

Get the life you want. Richard Bandler has said the conscious mind is the part of the mind that analyzes, criticizes and thinks logically all day long. Your unconscious is the part of your mind controlling your bodily functions, like heartbeat and breathing. It is where all your memories are stored and where your wisdom, creativity and problem-solving capabilities reside. When you are sleeping, your conscious mind is resting, but your unconscious is dreaming wildly and continues to help you process what has happened during the day.

What we think and our self-concept are the two main things that determine whether we will succeed or not in life. Our unconscious mind is responsible also for all sorts of illusions and is to blame for the phenomenon of the placebo effect. Often, behavior is shaped by subtle pressure around us, but we do not recognize that pressure. According to self-perception theory, people decide what they like and dislike from watching their behavior in various situations. We assume our sense of who we are from our behavior. But, it is not too late to change your neurology and head in the best direction for you; you have to activate your unconscious mind to align with your intention.

Are we what we believe we are? C.S. Lewis said, "we are what we believe we are." For example, if a child is stealing candy from grocery store, and no one notices him, the child does not change his self-perception that he is a good child. If the child gets caught and the parents make a big deal about it, The child may then think of himself as a thief. That may become the child's self-perception, and may become a self-fulfilling prophecy.

The unconscious mind has extraordinary power. The best example is muscular kinesiology. You have to take a leap of faith that your unconscious mind communicates with your muscles, and therefore has capacities for guiding healing, way beyond what we normally credit to the mind. Everyone has unconscious knowledge of what we need to heal. To access that knowledge, we need a way to enable the unconscious mind to speak. This is muscle kinesiology, the unconscious mind's capacity to access universal knowledge. (Susan Heitler)

Harnessing the power of the unconscious mind. By learning to influence the unconscious mind, you can make some pretty drastic breakthroughs. Even if you do not realize it, your unconscious mind runs the show in your life. It helps determine how much money you earn, how happy and successful you are, and what you believe to be true about the world. It affects how much you trust your partner, or how you see your place in the world. In short, your unconscious mind dramatically shapes your experience of life. But, the good news is with a bit of time and practice, it is totally possible to influence and reprogram your unconscious mind.

The difficulty is communicating with the mind in its language. It is like using Mandarin to speak to a Dutchman. You have to communicate in the same language of the unconscious mind. The language of the unconscious mind is emotion and images. So, when you experience positive emotions, form an image or picture so you can influence your unconscious mind. Bad programs and beliefs are installed when we experience powerful negative emotions, coupled with a big bold picture. So the key to influencing your unconscious mind is to feed it a compelling, bright picture of you at your best, and make it believable. Then you are speaking the same language as the unconscious mind.

The unconscious mind is neutral. If you dwell on past failures, the unconscious mind responds to that. Instead, keep your past and future successes in the front of your mind. Get excited about what the future holds. Feel confident, and over time your unconscious mind will dramatically change. The body of research tells us the unconscious mind has difficulty telling the difference between real and imagined or fake memory. Therefore, we may use this glitch in the matrix to our best advantage by sheer imagination. Consequently, those imagined images become part of our unconscious mind and help keep the negative events of life from dictating our personality.

Chapter Six

Ghost In the Machine

In the middle of the 20ᵗʰ century, there was a concept that the human mind is the product of a "ghost in the machine", and not the result of electrochemical interactions among neurons. If so, then the mind should not be dependent on the configuration of the brain that houses it. In short, there should be aspects of the mind that owe nothing to the physical function of the brain.

In British philosopher Gilbert Ryle's description of Rene Descartes' mind-body dualism, he introduces the concept of the mind. He rejected the idea that mental processes are separate from the body. The doctrine that was prevalent then among psychologists and philosophers was that every human being has both a body and mind. The body and the mind are ordinarily harnessed together, but after the death of the body, the mind may continue to exist and function.

Ryle states that the doctrine is unsound and conflicts with entire body. He says, "according to the official doctrine each person has direct and unchangeable cognizance." He indicated the then-accepted concept is entirely wrong and baseless.

Arthur Koestler wrote a book to answer Ryle's concept, titled *Ghost in the Machine*, which states that mankind moves toward self-destruction, particularly in the nuclear arms arena. The structure of the mind can overpower highly logical function, and is responsible for hate, anger and other such destructive impulses.

Rene Descartes' theory of mind-body dualism suggested the existence of a material body and an immaterial mind parallel to one another, but capable of communication via a metaphysical line. He envisioned our bodies as a biological locomotive, operated by other worldly phantoms. This concept of an immaterial realm, which somehow holds sway over the physical, is ubiquitous among cultures.

We crave explanations for what we observe, which in part gives rise to the smorgasbord of religious mythologies and elaborate metaphysical speculation, as the ghost in the machine unravels the mystery of our consciousness.

Contemporary neuroscience follows Descartes in conceptualizing consciousness as something that occurs internally. The difference is that for Descartes, the soul was a ghost in the machine, while for neuroscience the ghost is the machine. Until recently, this prediction was difficult to test, but modern scientific innovations have thrown light on the subject. Medical techniques such as CAT scans (computed axial tomography) or PET scans (position emission topography), and MRIs (magnetic resonance imaging) allow the structure and function of the living brain to be studied. Scientists can see which areas of the brain "light up" with activities when a healthy person performs mental tasks. Or, they can examine patients who have suffered injury or disease, to see which parts of the brain, when damaged, correspond to deficits of neural functions.

A disappointing result from theorists has emerged. Some mental functions are localized, while others are more diffused, but there is no aspect of the mind that does not correspond to any area of the brain. In fact, we know precisely which brain regions control many fundamental aspects of human consciousness. With the understanding that there is no mind-body dualism, comes the realization that the mind is, just as everything else, subject to the laws of nature, and to the infinite chain of cause and effect. This necessarily makes choice a very useful illusion, crucial even, but technically just a mirage.

Sam Harris in his book *The Moral Landscape* describes that all behavior can be traced to biological events about which we have no conscious knowledge. This suggests that free will is an illusion. The physiologist Benjamin Livet demonstrated that activity in the brain's motor regions can be detected some 350 milliseconds before a person feels that he has decided to move. Another lab recently used FMRI data to show that some conscious decisions can be predicted up to 10 seconds before they enter awareness. Findings of this kind are difficult to reconcile with the sense that you are the conscious source of your actions.

<u>Philosophies of the mind</u>. It is said the main defining characteristic of a person is consciousness, mind, or soul. We are all aware of our consciousness (feelings, thoughts, and sensations.) Plato thought we are really a soul, and this soul will survive after death. Indeed death is seen as the release of the soul. The body and soul are distinct substances; bodies die, but souls are immortal. Aristotle thought that body and soul are essentially related. T.H.Huxley supported epiphenomenalism. He saw the mind as the product of materials. For example, if I think I want some chocolate, it may be my stomach sending a message to the brain, because my blood sugar level is low. An epiphenomenalism consciousness has no power to cause anything; it is simply a reflection of biology, and of course when the body dies, the mind dies with it.

Descartes, the father of modern philosophy reopened the debate with his dualism view. He used his famous method of doubt. As doubting involves thoughts, and thought needs a consciousness to think it, he could not doubt the existence of his mind -- cogito ergo sum (I think, therefore I am.) He called it dualism because mind and body are separate and distinct. The mind is conscious and non-spatial and the body is spatial but not conscious, and both interact via the pineal gland.

Identity theory by Spinoza suggested mind and body are different; the mind is the brain and the brain is the mind. Consciousness is the individual's experiences of the brain, and a scientist can observe brain processes that correspond to conscious experiences. To illustrate, think of a pain. If you stub your toe, you will be aware of pain on physical level. Your central nervous system is sending messages from your toe to your brain. Or, suppose you want to raise your arm. Your decision to move your body sends messages from your brain to your muscles and your arm moves. This is fine when it comes to pain and simple movement; things become more complicated if you think of freedom or traveling.

Behaviorism rejects the concept of the mind altogether, and can only deal with the observable. As the mind is not observable, then nothing can be said about it. Behaviorist psychologists are not denying consciousness, but they say from their perspective they can analyze behavior only.

Gilbert Ryle talked about Descartes' ghost in the machine concept, and said confusion about mind and body arises by the way we use the word <u>mind</u>. For example, when we refer to someone as intelligent, then we are, in fact, making a judgment about that person's behavior; they acted intelligently on a particular occasion. Thus, intelligence is not a private entity.

For most of us, what is interesting about the mind or consciousness is our awareness of it, rather than our behavior. It is not clear that all mental states have a corresponding behavior. What behavior is associated with hearing a tune, or remembering an old friend? From the point of view of an observer, behavior is associated with types of mental activity.

Chapter Seven

Establishing the Paradigm of Our Thoughts

A paradigm is a pattern or model, how something is structured, or the lens through which we view ourselves and the world around us. It is thoughts turned into images and stored in our unconscious mind. It comes from the Greek word *pardeigmia*, which means a pattern of thoughts. A paradigm is repeated over and over and becomes part of our mindset. It is like a language. How do we learn a language? We are around people who speak Arabic or Russian, then we learn the language. It's just a matter of repetition, and that's how we establish our paradigm.

Once established, it tends to dictate logic, and have almost total control over our behavior. It is the little voice inside of us; the habits we formulate. Thus, a paradigm can be multitudes of habits ingrained and fixed in our unconscious mind. Habits are fixed ideas we act upon. We cannot break away from them, but we can replace them with other habits. That, of course, is a great challenge to us.

A paradigm is our pattern of thinking. It is our mindset, our ideas about us, and the world around us. It is a system of habits that your brain has developed over several years. It is the operating system on which your mental process runs. Your paradigm creates the prism through which most people view and make sense of the world around them. Information is presented to your mind in one way or another. Your mind runs through all of the things it already knows about that piece of information, and figures out where it fits in with the bigger picture.

Then your mind makes a determination whether the information is good or bad, desirable or undesirable, possible or not possible, all of which can be influenced by your existing paradigm. Paradigms, in and of themselves, are neutral. If your paradigm is positive, you will have a happy, growth-oriented life, a healthy self-image, and the ability to adapt successfully to change. Conversely, a negative paradigm can keep you stuck in old ways of thinking that can be very limiting. A negative paradigm keeps you a prisoner in your own cell, preventing you from positive growth. Thus, if you want any change you have to change your paradigm first, and get released from your own imprisonment. The majority of us experience some degree of imprisonment, either by our culture, our established beliefs, or by our biased experiences.

Why do we believe what we believe? Beliefs are ingrained in us from the time we were children, by our mother, father, teachers, preacher and society. Then we carry all of those beliefs into adulthood. They govern how we behave or act, and the minute details of life.

Nevertheless, changing your reality means changing your paradigm. To change your paradigm you have to change your habits. Habits are formed by repetition. The more we practice new habits, the less time we have to practice old habits. Sandra Gallagher said changing your self-image is the most important thing you can do to change your current reality or paradigm. Remember, you are using the same intellectual faculties that everyone else has, like Bill Gates, Bill Clinton, or other outstanding people. But the difference between you and them is simply that they have a more powerful image of themselves than you do. It also depends on what you want for your life. You can tap into your self-image and use your mental tools in the right way to change your paradigm.

Unfortunately, generally speaking, most people do not use their imaginations effectively. Instead of visualizing what they want, they create an image of themselves that keeps them right where they are. You might think you already know all of this. But what you need to do is create an image of what you want, not what you do not want, and you keep this image alive in your mind and consistently nurture it. Then it will manifest in your life.

According to Bob Proctor, all of the great leaders down through history have told us that we become what we think about. In fact, they have been in complete and unanimous agreement on this point, while they disagree on almost every other point. Unfortunately, the vast majority of people rarely think, they simply accept what they see or hear. The next time someone gives you an idea, rather than simply accepting and acting on it, think it, and exercise your reasoning ability. Ask yourself if the idea will improve the quality of your life.

When you use an excuse for not accomplishing something or not completing a project, you are actually giving power to something outside of yourself. Regardless of what happens today, absolutely refuse to use an excuse to get off the hook. Just challenge yourself, so you can change your paradigms. The reward can be immense satisfaction.

We are programmed since birth, according to Dr. Bruce Lipton, and the most influential perceptual programming of the unconscious mind occurs from birth through age six. During that time, the child's brain is recording all sensory experiences as well as learning complex motor programs for speech, crawling, standing, and advanced activities like running and jumping. Simultaneously, the child's sensory systems are fully engaged, downloading massive amounts of information about the world and how it works.

By observing the behavioral patterns of people in their immediate environment -- primarily parents, siblings and relatives -- children learn to distinguish acceptable and unacceptable social behavior. It is important to realize that perceptions acquired before the age of six become fundamentally the unconscious programs that shape character later on. We know in this stage the brain downloads massive amounts of cultural information, and becomes part of powerful unconscious materials.

The Childhood Paradigm. If we study brain waves, the brain frequencies in a developing child display a radically different behavior. The predominant brain activity during the first two years of life is delta, the lowest EEG frequency range. Between age two and six, the brain activity ramps up and operates primarily in the range of theta waves. In the theta state children spend much of their time mixing the imaginary world with the real world. The predominant delta and theta brain activity expressed by children younger than six signifies their brains are operating at levels below consciousness. Delta and theta brain frequency define a brain state known as the hypnotic trance stage, the same neural state a hypnotherapist uses to directly download new behavior into the subconscious mind. In other words, the first six years of child's life are effectively spent in a hypnotic trance.

This has a lasting effect upon our personality; this why we have to nurture our children with love and caring so we can have a happy society later on. If we see suffering or lack of progress in any society, it's because that society did not pay attention to childhood. That is what we see in the Arab world. Childhood is almost ignored; therefore, Arabs do not have a healthy society, as children are traumatized by ignorant and tyrannical parents, as well as the society.

A child's perceptions of the world are directly downloaded into the unconscious during this time, without discrimination and without filtering by the analytical self-conscious mind which does not fully exist. Consequently, our fundamental perceptions about life and our role in it are learned without having the capacity to choose or reject those beliefs. Simply we were programmed, and once programmed, information inevitability influences 95% of an individual's behavior for the rest of his or her life, due to the absence of conscious processing, which is alpha EEG activity.

There is a very serious consequence and downside to acquiring information this way, because we download our perception and beliefs about life before we acquire the ability for critical thinking. As a young child we download limiting or sabotaging beliefs. Those perceptions become our truth, and our behavior later on matches early learning.

By now you may think, I am not a victim of genetic programming. It now appears I am a victim of environmental programming. But, the programming can be reversed and reprogrammed, because the self-conscious mind endows organisms with one of the most powerful forces in the universe: the opportunity to express free will. It requires a lot of dedication and serious energy to transform our life, and overcome the early programming.

These are brain activities seen through the EEG:

Activities	Frequency	Brain State
Delta	0.5-4 HZ	Sleeping/Unconscious
Theta	4-8 HZ	Imagination State
Alpha	8-12 HZ	Calm/Consciousness
Beta	12-35 HZ	Focused Consciousness
Gamma	More than 35 HZ	Peak Performance

Once we establish the frame of our thoughts, it is through thinking that humans have what we have in life. Thinking is the movement of ideas in the mind to come to a definite conclusion. Our experiences are created in accordance with our beliefs, behind the ideas on which the thoughts was formed and contained in our conclusions. Of course, all these thoughts are unconscious.

We need to pay attention to the delta and theta brain waves, because those stages are the foundation of our personality later in life. We have to be extremely careful what we say or how we behave toward our children, because they internalize everything and it becomes an essential part of the fabric of their personality. Either we give them the positive, nurturing messages through which we eventually create a happy society, or show them the negative part of life. That will lead to unhappy people, and eventually an unhappy society, and we may struggle later on to change the already established paradigm, which can be a monumental job.

Chapter Eight

The Mind - Body Relationship

The brain is a physical object made of atoms, while the mind is a brain in action. If we reason this out, we find there is no contact between the mind and matter. When you understand that objects are just reflections in the mind, you realize what your mind comprehends is not the objects themselves, but merely images or pictures. The mind is not a fixed thing with some permanence, but a process. The mind is moving, because it is dynamic. The mind does not exist as a tangible substance; it is not a physically existing thing. The mind is not limited by size, shape, or color.

Buddha defined the mind as a non-physical phenomenon which perceives, thinks, recognizes, experiences, and reacts to the environment. It is like a mirror; it can clearly reflect objects. It has two main aspects: clarity and knowing. The mind is clear, formless and allows objects to rise to the surface, along with knowing, considered an awareness, a consciousness which can engage with objects.

The mind and body are powerful allies. How you think, can affect how you feel. And how you feel can affect your thinking. The interaction between them can affect personal health. The best example is the digestive system, which is profoundly controlled by the mind. Anxiety, depression, and fear dramatically affect the function of the digestive system. For instance, Irritable Bowel Syndrome can cause excruciating pain, and it can be caused by nervous thoughts. The best treatment is to heal the mind, or wean it from negative drastic thoughts.

Psychological stress can also trigger or aggravate a wide variety of diseases and disorders, such as diabetes, high blood pressure, and migraine headaches. Emotion can affect certain bodily functions, such as heart rate, blood pressure, perspiration, sleep patterns, stomach acid secretions, and bowel movements.

There is a pathway between the brain and the immune system. Research has shown that the brain communicates with white blood cells. For example, depression may suppress the immune system, and make a person susceptible to infections and viruses like the common cold.

Mind-body interaction is a two way street. Not only do psychological factors contribute to the onset, or aggravate a wide variety of physical disorders, but physical disease can affect a person's thinking or mood. People with a chronic disease commonly become depressed. The depression may also worsen the effect of physical disease and add to a person's misery. In 1930, Walter Cannon and his colleagues talked about mind-body medicine, and measured the relationship between life events and illness. They showed clinical improvement in patients treated with a placebo for a variety of illness. The effectiveness of placebo treatments can be interpreted as compelling evidence that expectation and belief can affect physiological response. Thus, mind-body interaction can be real and measured by electroencephalography (EEG). For example, mapping the relaxation response, shows the change in mental activity that can create a change in central nervous system activity.

Philosophers view the mind as immaterial information in the brain; they see the mind as software in the brain's hardware. They also see the relationship as a classic dualism, meaning we have distinction between essence and existence, between universal and particular, between eternal and ephemeral.

The best example of the mind-body connection is how the body responds to stress. Constant worry and stress over jobs, finances, or other problems can cause tense muscles, pain, headaches, and stomach problems. It may also lead to high blood pressure or other serious problems. On the other hand, constant pain or a health problem like heart disease can affect your emotions. You might become depressed, anxious, and stressed, which could affect how well you treat, manage, or cope with illness. But, the mind can have a positive affect on your health. Once you have a positive outlook on life with better skills to handle pain and stress, it will lead to a strong immune system to fend off most illness.

How thoughts can affect the body. The brain produces endorphins, which are painkillers that improve health. For example, even if you are sick, but with a positive outlook, you will get better, and heal sooner than a person with a negative outlook. The brain produces a chemical that boosts our immune system. There is a complex interrelationship between the mind and the body. Dr. James Gordon states that the mind and body are essentially inseparable. The brain and peripheral nervous system, the endocrine and immune system, all the organs of our body and all the emotional responses we have share a common chemical language and are constantly in communication with each other.

Regarding physical occurrence and mental process interaction, step barefoot on a tack, and you will feel a sharp pain. Or imagine you are waiting for a loved one at the station. The whistle of the approaching train makes your heart race in anticipation. This would probably never happen if you are waiting in the station for casual friend. Thus, our thoughts, desires, and feelings are regularly followed by a change in body chemistry and neural activities. Often, we predict what effect having certain thoughts will have on our bodies.

Perception and Sensation. The first channel of interaction between the body and the mind is sensation, where the world stimulates the body through the sense organs, to enable perception. To stimulate is to connote the event where the world activates the sensory capacity of a person; e.g., when light hits the eyes, sound vibrates the eardrums, or objects pass across the skin. Sensation, subsequently, is the channel by which sensory information is passed to the mind. Thus, we treat sensation as a relation between the body and mind. It has two possibilities: either active or inactive, to differentiate based on the state of sensation.

The mind-body debate. The mind is about mental processes, consciousness and thoughts. The body is about the physical aspects of the brain -- the nervous system and how the brain is structured. But, is the mind part of the body, or is the body part of the mind? If they are distinct, then how do they interact? And which of the two is in charge? There are many theories put forward to explain the relationship. You experience your thoughts and your brain is part of your body. Thus, human beings are material objects; we have weight, solidity and consist of a variety of solids, liquids, and gases Unlike other material objects (e.g. rocks) humans also have the ability to form judgments and reason our existence, so we have the mind as well.

Typically, humans are characterized as having both a mind and body; this is called dualism. However, there are two types of dualism: A) Descartes' dualism, the view that mind and body function separately without exchange; and B) Cartesian dualism, the view that there is a two-way interaction between mental and physical substances. There is also monism, which says the body and mind are the same thing. There are two types of monism: Materialism, which believes nothing exists apart from the material world (physical matter), like the brain. They believe the mind is the brain in action, meaning the mind is a function of the brain. Mental processes can be identified with purely physical processes in the central nervous system, and human beings are just complicated physiological organisms, no more than that. Phenomenalism, or subjective idealism, believes physical objects and events are reducible to mental objects, properties, and events. Ultimately, only mental objects exist.

The human mind is the most highly evolved form of the biological information processing that goes on in all organisms. We usually think our mind is in control, and tells our body what to do. However, there is a lot of scientific evidence that shows the chatter between mind and body goes two ways. The body is an integral part of how we think, and surely the body influences our psyche.

One landmark study showed clear evidence of the mind-body connection, and the impact of meditation. A group working out of Alberta Health Services, the Tom Baker Cancer Center, and the University of Calgary Dept. of Oncology demonstrated that telomeres -- protein complexes at the end of chromosomes -- maintain their length in breast cancer survivors who practice meditation or are involved in support groups, while they shorten in a comparison group without any intervention. The disease-regulating properties of telomeres are not fully understood; however, shortened telomeres are associated with several disease states, as well cell aging, while longer telomeres are thought to be protective against disease. Dr. Linda E. Carlson, principal researcher, determined that mindful meditation will help you feel better mentally. But for the first time we have evidence that it can also influence a key aspect of our biology. Over a 3-month period, it was surprising to see a difference in telomere length at all.

Chapter Nine

The Biology of Thoughts

In the biological brain, our goals are established by the inherited pleasure and fear centers. These primitive drives were initially set by biological evolution to foster the survival of the species, but the neocortex has enabled us to sublimate them.

How do thoughts change your brain? Every thought creates a neural connection. If you think a thought often enough the neural connection will grow strong, particularly if there is an emotion attached to it. Conversely, if a memory has little use, is rarely stimulated, or has no emotional attachment, eventually those neural connections will largely wither away from disuse.

Thought also changes your brain by stimulating the production of brain chemicals which can change the structure and function of your brain. A good example is what happens to your brain under stress. When a situation you perceive as stressful occurs, it increases your level of the stress hormone cortisol. Prolonged exposure to cortisol literally excites some of your brain cells to death. Particularly in the hippocampus, where memories are stored, this can cause measurable shrinkage of this part of the brain. That's why people who are under constant stress become forgetful and lack concentration.

Conversely, stress feeds the amygdala, your fear center, causing it to grow, leaving you more fearful and anxious. Excess cortisol halts the formation of brain-derived neurotropic factor (BDNF), a protein which acts like fertilizer to encourage the growth of new brain cells. Research suggests that chronic stress stimulates the protein that might even be the cause of Alzheimer's Disease.

Scientists have made progress observing the brain in action and determining how groups of neurons function. They pinpointed hubs in the brain that are responsible for certain tasks, such as fleeing a dangerous situation, processing visual information, or creating dreams, as well as making strong long-term memories. But understanding the mechanism of how neuronal networks collaborate to allow such tasks has remained more elusive. According to Weinberger, we do not yet have a good way to study how groups of neurons form functional networks.

For example, when we learn, remember, or do anything else, including seeing, hearing, moving, or loving, we really do not understand how these clusters of brain cells somehow give rise to more complex behavior and emotions, such as altruism, sadness, empathy and anger. We can identify the region in the brain that made Mother Teresa altruistic, but we are unable to identify what drove her altruism.

How much of your brain do you actually need? Apparently, you could get along well with as little as half of it if necessary. Experiments on soldiers who suffered penetrating head wounds during World War II showed when those men were retested for intelligence, they showed little or no change in the score they had achieved in the Army General Classification Test, upon first entering the service some 10 years earlier. There is a belief that the brain is highly compartmentalized, with specific areas for specific functions, but recent studies indicate when a specific area is damaged, another brain area may be able to take over its function, with human intelligence capacity continuing virtually unimpaired. This is where neuron plasticity plays a major role in making up for the missing functions. There is also a close relationship between intelligence and hand dexterity.

Can we really learn while we are sleeping? Research by Dr. C.W. Simon and W.H. Emmond indicates that learning is possible during a drowsy state but not during actual sleep. As far as brain capacity, brain weight at birth is only about 12 ounces and in an adult about three pounds, with a few ounces more in men than in women. Storage capacity is phenomenal.

Is there any relationship between baldness and the brain? This theory, recently offered by Dr. Wharton Young, professor of anatomy at Howard University, will be flattering to all men and especially to those who are bald. It holds that in men the brain is constantly growing, expanding the cranium and stretching the top of the scalp so that the fat layer under the scalp is squeezed, depriving the hair roots of adequate blood and nourishment. This can reach a point where the hair falls out. Women keep their hair because their brain is smaller and grows more slowly.

Most scientists agree that men and women are fairly equal in mental ability. However, there are specific differences between the sexes. A Stanford University study for the Office of Naval Research showed that other factors being equal, men are as much as 50% better than women in solving complicated problems.

The biological structure of the brain. We have roughly 86 billion neurons in our brain, but unlike common theory, we do not just use 10% of them; we use most of them all the time. Neurons are cells in the brain that convey information about the world around us, help us make sense of the world, and send commands to our muscles to act. They are inquisitively responsive to the world around us, and enable us to learn. Learning can change the shape of neurons, what the neuron connects to, and its signaling efficiency. Most neurons are made up of a nucleus, which contains genetic instructions; the soma, or cell body; dendrites, branch-like structures which receive information from other neurons; and the axom, a long tubular pathway which sends information to other parts of the brain.

Neurons have a pre-synaptic terminal, which connects to other neurons through synapses. If a neuron responds to a stimulus, its axon sends an all-or-nothing electrical signal called an action potential to its axonal terminal. Action potentials are the way the brain receives, processes, and conveys information.

Neurons come in many shapes and sizes, but most resemble differently-shaped trees; human neurons can be as small as 10 ums (one thousandth of a millimeter), and as large as 100 ums (one tenth of a mm). The brain contains other cells, called glia, which serve numerous supporting functions, including repairing damage following brain injury, and aiding in metabolic pathways which modulate neuron function.

For decades, it was held that humans could not generate new neurons as an adult. Now we know that humans, like other species, can grow new neurons, but only in certain parts such as the hippocampus, which is involved in memory.

Is there a close relationship between genius and insanity? Not necessarily, but there is a higher incidence of psychoneurosis than in the general population, and normally geniuses are the first or second born. There is also a relationship between artists and depression.

Wiring. A neuron by itself cannot do much. It is a starting point. The connections between neurons and between neurons, muscles, and other effector organs make our brain work. It is the connection of many simpler neurons into a higher-order cell which enables us to process more complex information. And it is the multiple unique connections between certain sets of neurons that create functional neuronal circuits or pathways. Broadly, the brain contains both sensory and motor pathways.

During development, neurons in the brain are over wired; numerous connections are made between cells. As the infant and child learn through experiences, the connection is pruned. Some of these connections are strengthened, others die. These neurons carry messages through electrochemical processes.

The existence of the mind is divided into two classes: Matter and Mind. These are distinguished from each other by their qualities. Matter is that which has the qualities of figure, is divisible, extension, inertia and attraction. Mind is that which thinks, feels and wills. The science which treats these various phenomena of matter is called natural science. The science which treats of the phenomena of mind is called mental philosophy.

The most general classification of mental phenomena, the common language of life, divides the operations of the mind into the three general classes: thoughts, feelings and choice. Thoughts dominate understanding, reasoning powers, intellect, and intellectual powers. Feelings are considered affection, susceptibilities of the heart, and the active powers.

Choice is called the will, and it can be classed among the feelings, attractions, or intellectual power. All of these generate specific acts of mind, such as sensation, perception, conception, imagination, memory, association, attention, judgment, abstraction, and consciousness. For example, when light, considered a type of matter, affects the eye, the sensation of sight is produced, and so forth.

The primary functions of each part of the brain. The *frontal lobe* controls initiation, problem solving, judgment, inhibition of behavior, self-monitoring, personality, awareness of abilities and limitations, attention, concentration, organization, expression and motor planning. The *parietal lobe* covers the sense of touch, along with shape, color, and visual and spatial perception. The *occipital lobe* controls vision.

The *cerebellum* controls balance, coordination of skill, and motor activity. In other words, it regulates movement. The *temporal lobe* covers memory, hearing, understanding language, organization and sequencing. Breathing, hearing, arousal, sleep and wake cycles, attention and consciousness are functions of the *brain stem*. It sends neuromodulators like serotonin and dopamine to the rest of the brain.

The *anterior (frontal) cingulated cortex* (ACC) involves attention and monitoring plans, integrates thinking and feelings. The *cingulated cortex* is a curved bundle of nerve fibers. Other areas of the brain and their functions include:

The *insula* oversees the interior state of your body, including hurt feelings, and helps with empathy. It is located inside the temporal lobes on each side of your head, along with the *thalamus*, a station for sensory information. The *corpus callosum* passes information between the two hemispheres of the brain. The *limbic system* is central for emotion and motivation, and includes the basal ganglia, hippocampus, hypothalamus, and pituitary gland. *Basal ganglia* are involved with the reward system, as well as stimulation to seek.

The *hippocampus* forms new memory and detects threats, and the *amygdala* is the alarm for emotions. The *hypothalamus* regulates primary drives such as hunger and sex, and makes oxytocin to activate the pituitary gland. The *pituitary gland* produces endorphins, triggers stress hormones, and stores and releases oxytocin.

There are also major chemicals inside our brain that affect neural activities and functions:

Glutamate excites receiving neurons; *GABA* inhibits receiving neurons.

Serotonin regulates mood, sleep, and digestion. Most anti-depressants aim at increasing its effects. *Dopamine* is the key neurotransmitter for reward and attention. The brain also produces *Opioids*, which tend to soothe and reduce pain, and produce pleasure.

Norepinephrine is a neurotransmitter that makes you alert and arouses you. *Acetylcholine* promotes wakefulness and learning. *Oxytocin* promotes nurturing behavior toward children, and helps to form a bond between men and women, but women have more of it. It is a very essential neurotransmitter to develop intimacy between a couple.

Vasopressin supports bonding in men and aggression toward rivals. *Estrogen* is in both sexes, and promotes libido, mood and memory.

Cortisol is released by the adrenal glands during a stress response. It stimulates the amygdala and inhibits the hippocampus. It tends to shrink the hippocampus, which is why we become forgetful as a result of stress hormones.

It increases the size of amygdale, which makes us prone for more stress and jumpy behavior. Thus, people in poverty or in an oppressive culture tend to be aggressive, short tempered, anxious, devious, and angry, because the oppression of the culture increases the size of the amygdale.

The human brain, like other vertebrates, is divided into three regions: A) the Hindbrain; B) Midbrain; and C) Forebrain, plus the spinal cord which makes up our central nervous system. The Hindbrain contains the cerebellum, an important site for integration of sensory and motor input. The Midbrain's main structure is the optic tectum, which receives visual input along with other senses, including sound, and controls eye movement. The Forebrain houses the cerebral cortex, which contains the thalamus and the hypothalamus, which regulate hormonal and autonomic responses. The occipital lobes, in the back of our head, receive visual input from the eyes and process the images through multiple maps. The Parietal lobes are the site for somatosensory information. The Temporal lobes are for sound and language, while the Frontal lobes are the site for the motor cortex which guides voluntary movement.

Chapter Ten

Neuroplasticity

Our brain was constructed for change. As Marguerite Holloway said, "score one for believers in the adage, use it or lose it." Targeted mental and physical exercises seem to improve the brain in an unexpected way. This may seem an obvious idea as our brain revises as we learn. The "use it or lose it" adage is very applicable here.

Today we talk in a more profound way, about the brain being extensively remodeled throughout the course of one's life without drugs or surgery. Regions of the brain can be taught to do different tasks if needed to. If one area has dysfunction or damage, another can step in and play that role, thereby shifting the tasks of the damaged area to another.

Only a few decades ago, scientists considered the brain to be fixed or hardwired, and therefore considered most forms of brain damage to be incurable. Now, it's understood that the brain changes its very structure with each different activity performed. If one part of the brain fails, other parts may take over. This process is called neuroplasticity. The nerve cells in our brains and nervous system are like plastic: changeable, malleable and modifiable.

Other scientists have shown that thinking, learning, and acting can turn our genes on and off. Thus, shaping our brain anatomy, and thus our behavior, is surely one of the most extraordinary discoveries of the 20th century.

The science of the mind today can work with people who do not see and try to make them see, or help those with brain damage to walk, or work with the elderly who have memory trouble, and can reverse it to act as if they are 20 years old. The neuroplasticity revolution has implications for, among other things, our understanding of how love, sex, grief, relationships, learning, addictions, culture, technology, and psychotherapies all can change our brain.

Neuroplasticity is not all good news, as it may subject us to be vulnerable to outside influences. For example, if we develop habits that are echoed in our neurons, it may make it difficult for us to change such habits since it is "hard wired."

Neuroplasticity and the stages of development. In 1868, the idea of one brain function, one brain location emerged through Jules Cotard, who studied children who had early massive brain disease, in which the left hemisphere wasted away. Yet these children could still speak normally. This meant that even though speech was processed in the left hemisphere, the brain might be plastic enough to reorganize itself, if necessary. In 1876, Otto Soltmann removed the motor cortex, the part of the brain thought to be responsible for movement, from infant dogs and rabbits, yet found they were still able to move. This finding has suggested that the idea of one function one location was not valid.

In another study in 1960, a team of scientists in Germany studied how vision worked by measuring with electrodes the electrical discharge from the visual processing area of a cat's brain. The team fully expected that when they showed the cat an image, the electrode in its visual processing area would send off an electric spike, showing it was processing that image. And it did, but when the cat's paw was accidentally stroked, the visual area also fired, indicating that it was processing touch as well. They also found the visual area was active when the cat heard sounds.

In 1985, Turner and Greenough found that animals raised in an enriched environment, for example surrounded by other animals, objects to explore, toys to roll, ladders to climb, and running wheels, learn better. The animals had more acetylcholine, a brain chemical essential for learning, heavier and thicker neocortexes, larger neurons with more dendrites, and more synaptic connections than animals raised in deprived environments.

Perhaps, this is why some societies are more advanced than others. If they are impoverished, or have an oppressive culture with no music, art, theater, and cinema, these activities nurture the sense of beauty and appreciation of life. Thus, neuroplasticity can play a major role and is crucial in brain development, because an enriched environment stimulates brain growth, and forms new synaptic connections. The brain is like any other muscle in our body; it tends to grow when you provide it with the proper exercise.

Merzenich has made the claim in the field of neuroplasticity, that exercising the brain may be as effective or useful as drugs to treat certain diseases, because plasticity exists from the cradle to the grave. That can cause radical improvement in cognitive functioning, which is how we learn, think, perceive, and remember even in our old age. He argues that practicing a new skill, under right conditions, can change hundreds of millions and possibly billions of connections between the nerve cells in our brain maps.

Furthermore, the cerebral cortex, the thin outer layer of the brain is actually selectively refining its processing capacities to fit each task at hand. It does not simply learn, it is always learning how to learn. Merzenich added that the brain is not a vessel to be filled; rather it is more like a living creature with an appetite that can grow and change itself with proper nourishment and exercise. Before Merzenich's work the common belief was the brain is a complex machine, having unalterable limits on memory, processing speed and intelligence. But all these assumptions have lately been shown to be incorrect.

Dr. Wilder Penfield of Montreal has mapped the brain by touching each area and asking the patient for the corresponding sensation, localizing the activities of the brain. He discovered the frontal lobes were the seat of the brain's motor system, which initiates and coordinates muscle movement, and the other three lobes behind the frontal lobe -- the temporal, parietal, and occipital -- comprise the brain sensory system, and processing signals sent to the brain from sensory receptors such as the eyes, ears, and touch receptors.

A later study by Hubel and Wiesel examined the brain map of a kitten with a blind eye. They discovered the plasticity of the kitten's brain. The part which had been deprived of input from the shut eye did not remain idle. It had begun to process visual input from the open eye, as though the brain did not want to waste any cortical real estate. It found a way to rewire itself, which is another indication of brain neuroplasticity. Both of those scholars received the Nobel Prize, for their great contribution to the field of neuroplasticity

Another outstanding study by ethnologist Konrad Lorenz observed if you expose goslings to humans after their birth, from three days to a few hours a day, they tend to bond to humans instead of their biological mother. He had a group of goslings following him around. This process is called imprinting. Freud said in a brief window of time we need to go through certain experiences to be healthy and have a sound self-concept. This period is the formative stage of our life, and it shapes us for the rest of our life.

It is important to understand that the nervous system is divided into parts. The first part is the central nervous system, the brain and the spinal cord. This is the command-and-control center of the system, which was once believed to lack plasticity. The second part is the peripheral nervous system, which brings messages from the sense receptors to the spinal cord and brain, and carries messages from the brain and spinal cord to the muscles and glands. The peripheral nervous system was long known to have plasticity; if you cut a nerve in your hand, it can regenerate itself.

Neuroplasticity has changed medical practice profoundly. For example, children born with cataracts no longer face blindness because of corrective surgery, and neuroplasticity. Each neuron has three parts. The dendrites are treelike branches that receive input from other neurons. These dendrites lead to the cell body, which sustains the life of the cell and contains its DNA, and the axon, which has varying lengths. Axons are often compared to wires, because they carry electrical impulses at very high speeds.

However, plasticity has a competitive nature. There is an endless war of nerves going on inside the brain. If we stop exercising our mental skills, we do not just forget them, the brain map space for those skills is turned over to the skills we practice instead. If you ever ask yourself how often you must practice the guitar or study math to keep on top of it, you are asking a question about competitive plasticity, to make sure the brain map real estate for those skills is not lost to another activity. The brain has plasticity, yet it is hard to learn a new language, and end the tyranny of the mother tongue. Unlearning is often much harder than learning. Early childhood is therefore important, and it is best to get it right early, before bad habits get a competitive advantage.

Merzenich has demonstrated plasticity in a very simple, understandable way. He mapped the hand in the brain of a monkey. Then he amputated the monkey's middle finger. After a number of months he remapped the monkey brain and found the brain map for the amputated finger had disappeared and the maps for the adjacent fingers had grown into the space that had originally mapped for middle finger. This experiment showed that brain maps are dynamic, and this was the clearest possible demonstration of the principle "use it or lose it."

Merzenich also found that maps of normal body parts change every few weeks. Every time he mapped a normal monkey's face, it was clearly different. Thus, he concluded that plasticity is a normal phenomenon, and brain maps are constantly changing. He also argued that brain maps alter their border and location and change their functions well into adulthood. Localizationists, of course, opposed this idea. He also proposed that neurons in brain maps develop strong connections to one another when they are activated at the same moment in time. In another experiment he sewed two fingers of a monkey together and mapped the brain. After a few weeks he found the map of two fingers became one.

The application of this theory is critical for people born with certain problems, like learning difficulties, or stroke victims, or those with brain injuries. They might be able to form new maps if they are helped by forming new neuronal connections, getting their healthy neurons to fire together and wire together. However, autism, a pervasive developmental disorder which impacts intelligence, perception, social skills, language and emotion, is very baffling to the field of psychology.

Merzenich thinks the neglect of intensive learning as we age causes the system of the brain that modulates, regulates, and controls plasticity to waste away. In response he developed brain exercises for age-related cognitive decline -- the common decline of memory, thinking and processing speed.

Can we enlarge our brain, or are stuck with the brain that we have at birth? Merzenich continues to challenge that view, because the brain is structured by its constant collaboration with the world. It is not only the parts of the brain most exposed to the world, such as our senses, that are shaped by experiences. Plastic change, caused by our experiences, travels deep into the brain and ultimately even into our genes, molding them as well.

It is reasonable to ask whether sexual plasticity is related to neuroplasticity. Research has shown that neuroplasticity is not localized in a certain area or department in the brain, nor is it confined to the sensory, motor, or cognitive processing areas. The brain structure that regulates instinctive behaviors, including sex, is called the hypothalamus. It has plasticity, as does the amygdala, the structure that processes emotion and anxiety. While some parts of the brain, such as the cortex, have more plasticity potential because there are more neurons and connections to be altered, even neocortical areas display plasticity. It is a property of all brain tissues. Plasticity exists in the hippocampus (the area that turns our short-term memory to long term) as well in areas that control our breathing, process primitive sensations, and process pain. It exists in the spinal cord as well.

Freud and Plato argued that sexuality has plasticity. Freud laid the foundation for neuroscientific understanding of human sexuality, and romantic plasticity. One of the primary contributions of Freud regarding sexual plasticity, is that sexuality unfolds in stages, beginning in the infant's first passionate attachments to his/her parents. Freud learned from his patients and from the observations of other children, moreover, that early childhood, not puberty, was the first critical period for sexuality and intimacy. At six years of age, children are capable of passionate sexual feelings. He also discovered that sexual abuse of children is harmful, because it influences the critical period of sexuality in childhood, and may shape later attraction and thoughts about the opposite sex, or even themselves.

In general, children are needy, and typically develop passionate attachments to their parents. If the parents are warm, gentle, and reliable, the child will frequently develop a taste for that kind of relationship later on. If the parents are disengaged, cool, distant, self-involved, angry, ambivalent, or erratic, the child may seek out an adult mate who has similar tendencies as his or her parents. Thus, if early patterns of relatedness and attachment to others are problematic, they become wired in the brain, and can cause serious ramifications in the child's life, and spill over into adulthood, and make life difficult.

A landmark of neuroplasticity. One of the best known scientists of our time in neuroplasticity is Edward Taub, who lives in Birmingham, Alabama. His well-known experiments showed that stroke patients can be treated through neuroplasticity. He has trained people to use their paralyzed hands. The study showed 80% of stroke victims who lost arm function improved substantially. Even patients who had a severe chronic stroke showed significant improvement.

In his research. Dr. Taub demonstrated that brain plasticity is capable of reorganizing, regardless of how long ago the patient had the stroke, or how long they have lived with the disability. Another study by Jena University in Germany showed that after a stroke the brain map for an affected arm shrank by about half, so a stroke patient has only half the original number of neurons to work with. Thus, atrophy happens not just for the muscles, but also to the brain, because of lack of use. Once again, "use it or lose it."

Dr. Taub's basic training forces the patient to practice using their damaged arm or leg, and is incremental. This extraordinary practice after just two weeks, helps rewire the brain by triggering plastic change. In other words, new neurons have taken over the lost functions, and may be quite effective in replacing the lost neurons. This technique is called Constraint Induced Therapy.

Merzenich showed when the sensory input from a finger was cut off, the brain map changed typically in 1 to 2 millimeters of the cortex, which means brain neurons, when damaged, might send out small sprouts or branches to connect to other neurons, and had the ability to grow 1 to 2 millimeters to compensate.

Clinical application of neuroplasticity. We may use neuroplasticity to stop worries or obsessions. Worry begets worry, and the rituals involved in obsession may relate to magical beliefs and superstitions. The brain of the obsessive person does not turn the page or move on; his automatic gearshift does not work. There are three parts of the brain are involved in obsession: the *orbital frontal cortex*, which is part of the frontal lobe, that creates the mistaken feeling, then it sends a signal to the *cingulate gyrus*, which triggers the feeling of anxiety that something bad is going to happen. Then the *caudate nucleus* becomes sticky and does not allow our thoughts to flow. The brains of OCD patients show that all three areas in the brain are hyperactive, and lock the brain in constant suffering.

Schwartz developed a treatment for OCD by shifting the focus of the patient and effortful attention to activities that focus on something pleasant, or on pleasurable activities that trigger the release of dopamine. This rewards the new activity and consolidates, growing new neuronal connections. This new circuit can eventually compete with the older one, and according to the rule of "use it or lose it", eventually, the pathological behavior will weaken, and we have replaced bad habits with better ones.

Even the brain of the bird can go through plasticity. Dr. Fernando Nottebohm, bird specialist, in 1980 found that birdsong can change in every season. We learn from neurogenesis that a bird every season replaces their neurons with another set of neurons. The other study by Gage and Eriksson injected a marker in a terminally ill patient, and after death they found out that their brain recently formed baby neurons in their hippocampus. Thus, we learned from dying patients that living neurons form in us until the very end of lives.

The other outstanding experiment, conducted by Gage and his colleague Gerd Kempermann, raised aging mice in an enriched environment, filled with mice toys like balls, tubes, and running wheels for 45 days. When they examined their brains, a 15% increase in the volume of their hippocampus was found, and 40,000 new neurons had developed, compared to mice raised in standard cages.

The application of these experiments may show us why the Arab people are not creative enough. They are raised in the cage of their impoverished culture of oppression, lack of social justice, insults, lack of freedom, and a pathological obsession with sexuality and women.

Undoubtedly, Arab culture is obsessed with women; perhaps they have not resolved their Oedipal conflicts. There is not enough nurturing or love in the basic fabric of Arab society. Further study is needed to identify the pathology of the Arab, to find a remedy, and participate in the human community. Sadly, the Arab culture does not allow an individual to use their neurons in a creative manner. Thus people gradually lose their mental faculties, and become numb, or they may become shallow, with no depth in their personal or societal life.

Through these experiments by Dr. Gage and his colleagues, we now know if humans are raised in a rich environment, unconfined culturally, personally free, and made to feel worthwhile and contribute to society, then the individual tends to be creative. On the other hand, if humans are raised in an impoverished environment, with no mental stimulation, they tend to lose some of their neurons, which is, once again, if you do not use it, you will lose it.

Merzenich believed if we want to keep our brain fit, we must learn something new, rather than simply replaying already-mastered skills. It does not just increase the number of neurons; we also can extend their life. The shift in the brain, shifting processing areas from one lobe to another, is like a migration of functions. The more education we have, the more use of the frontal lobes, which means the more education we have, the more we create a cognitive reserve.

It has also been proven that physical exercise brings oxygen to the brain, and that helps generate new neurons. At any age, exercise stimulates your sensory and motor cortices and maintains your brain's balance system. Nothing speeds brain atrophy more than being immobilized in the same environment. Monotony undermines our dopamine and attention systems, and can be detrimental to maintaining brain plasticity. There are many people who have done remarkable work in old age. For example, Frank Lloyd Wright designed the Guggenheim Museum at 90, and Benjamin Franklin invented bifocals at 78. There are many other examples of people who have outstanding inventions in the later years of their lives. This is due to brain plasticity.

Chapter Eleven

Mirror Neurons

We wake up in the morning and we through life effortlessly. We brush our teeth, we get dressed, we have coffee. And, we look to the people around us and understand them and often we predict their behavior. Philosophers and psychologists through human history are baffled at how we understand each other. Our understanding of other people is due to the collection of special cells in the brain called mirror neurons. These are incredible miracles that play great roles in life. They are at the heart of how we navigate life. They bind us with each other, mentally and emotionally.

For example, we cry when we see sad movies, we get upset when we see child abuse. We have empathy for fictional or real characters. We know how they feel, and literally experience the same feelings ourselves. When we see someone kissing his lover, our brain neurons fire as if we are kissing ours. Likewise, when we see someone suffering or in pain, mirror neurons help us read facial expressions and actually make us feel the suffering or pain of the other person. These feelings are the foundation of empathy, and possible morality, deeply rooted in our biology.

When watching sports teams playing against each other, and you support one team against the other, when your team scores you tend to have a very emotional reaction. This is caused by mirror neurons, meaning you want to share your reaction with others. By watching, it is as if we are playing the game ourselves. We understand the player's actions because our brains have an area for those movements.

Mirror neurons provide a plausible neurophysiological explanation for complex forms of social cognition and interaction, by helping us recognize and understand the deepest motives behind those actions and the intentions of other individuals. Solid empirical evidence suggests the brain is capable of mirroring the deepest aspects of the minds of others. Labs around the world are accumulating evidence that social deficits, such as those associated with autism, may be primarily due to a dysfunction of mirror neurons. It is also suggested mirror neurons are important in imitating the violence we see in the media, and are important in social identification, such as political parties, branding or any other affiliation.

The human brain contains about eighty-five billion neurons, each of which can make contact with thousands, even tens of thousands, of other neurons. These contacts, or synapses, are the means by which neurons communicate with one another, and their number is staggering. However, the distinguishing factor in the brain of mammals is the neocortex. It is the most recently evolved of our brain structures.

It is the slight variation in experiments around the world that revealed the subtlety of these neurons, which opened the door to our understanding. They also showed there a tight correlation between action and perception. These are called strictly congruent mirror neurons, because they fire for identical actions, either performed or observed. For instance, a strictly congruent mirror neuron fires when a monkey grasps with a precision grip, and when the monkey sees somebody else grasping with a precision grip.

Other mirror neurons, however, show a less strict relationship between executed and observed actions. These are broadly congruent mirror neurons. They fire at the sight of an action that is not necessarily identical to the executed action, but achieves a similar goal. For instance, they fire when the monkey is grasping food with the hand and when the monkey is seeing somebody else putting food in the mouth.

With mirror neurons you may know what others are thinking. For example say you're in the kitchen, and you have an argument with your spouse. She reaches out for a cup; does she want to throw is at you, clean it, or does she want coffee? The most basic property of mirror neurons, firing for both the action of grasping a cup and the result of the grasping action, can be helpful for recognizing the actions of other people. Do mirror neurons differentiate between the action associated with different intentions? It depends on prior experiences.

Mirror neurons can be used as a tool. Take the case of the Japanese monkey who washes potatoes, a behavior that spread from one individual to the whole community. This famous case spawned significant debate on animals' behavior. Initially the behavior was taken as evidence that monkeys can imitate novel action. But, imitation requires that someone act and others observe. It seems while the first monkey washes the potatoes, the attention of observing monkeys is directed to the water.

The next time the observing monkey is close to water with a potato in her hand, a simple trial and error mechanism during the manipulation of the potatoes in the water helped animals learn how to wash the potato. Washing the potato has spread widely among all monkey communities in several islands of Japan, and has fostered considerable debate within the scientific community. Mirror neurons involve the recognition of manipulation and holding the potato. But their role in spreading this behavior is limited to this initial form of action recognition. This is called the one hundred monkeys phenomenon.

Eric Hoffer said "when people are free to do as they please, they usually imitate each other." Darwin talked about the imitation of honeybees, but in fact imitation is deemed a pervasive feature of human behavior. It has been demonstrated by developmental psychologist Andrew Meltzoff, who conducted experiments on newborns at 41 minutes. He found that babies imitate rudimentary facial gestures, even though they have not seen the gestures before. Thus, in reality imitation is not learning; it is mirror neurons. There is plenty of reciprocal imitation between parents and babies; in fact, this specific mechanism is a major factor in shaping or reinforcing mirror neurons in brain development.

Most mirror neuron research has used monkeys. Data from Parma University demonstrated the discharge of mirror neurons while the monkeys were performing grasping actions was approximately twice as strong as the discharge while they were simply observing the grasping. John Napier said if language was given to men to conceal their thoughts, a gesture's purpose was to disclose them. Often, we gesture when we talk on the phone, or when we talk to a blind person, even though he does not see them. David McNeill argues that gestures and language are one system; that gestures are an integral part of language as much as are words, phrases, and sentences.

Language is the manual of gestures. This thinking has dominated for centuries. Mirror neurons support this hypothesis for two reasons: the anatomical analogy between humans and area F5 of the macaque brain, where mirror neurons were discovered, and gestures, the origin of language. A compelling form of communication exists at the gesture level.

Humans are like chameleons; we instinctually imitate one another. We synchronize our bodies, our actions, and even the way we speak to each other. This phenomenon has been studied in a host of ways, from clever experiments to detailed observations of human behavior. As Elaine Hatfield and Richard Rapson put in their book *Emotional Contagion*, people imitate others' expressions of pain, laughter, smiling, affection, embarrassment, discomfort, disgust, and the like, in a broad range of situations. Mimicry is a communication act which conveys a rapid and precise nonverbal message to another person. The rapid and precise nonverbal synchrony we enjoy with each other has an emotional component. Mimicking others is not just a form of nonverbal communication; it helps us to perceive others' expressions in the first place.

There is also a convincing study showing a link between imitation and empathy. One of the findings is that couples have a higher facial similarity (they look more like each other) after 25 years of married life than they did when they were married. The effect also correlates with the quality of the marriage, the higher the quality, the higher the facial similarity. It is really no surprise. When we love, share, and live together for a long time, it makes us look more and more similar. The spouse becomes a second self.

Empathetic Neurons. Sir Arthur Conan Doyle said the features are given to man as the means by which he shall express his emotions. The challenge we have is how brain areas containing mirror neurons are connected to limbic areas concerned with emotion, all through the insula. Because brain regions talk to each other, a good place to start is with the anatomy of the organ, showing how they must be connected in some way to each other. The network of neuron connections is the most complicated system in the human body.

The core of mirror neurons is empathy. For example, if you watch someone who is sad, fearful, happy, angry, surprised, or disgusted, mirror neurons, the limbic system (particularly the amygdala) and the insula all respond to the facial expressions of the other person, and imitation takes place. Mirror neurons help us understand the emotion of other people by some form of inner imitation. According to this hypothesis of empathy, our mirror neurons fire when we see others expressing their emotions, as if we are the ones making facial expressions associated with such emotion.

Several experiments regarding the response of our mirror neurons to pain have been conducted, finding that the brain produces a full simulation of observed pain. We commonly think of pain as a fundamentally private experience, while our brain treats it as an experience to share with others. This neural mechanism is essential for building social ties. It is also very likely that these forms of resonance with the painful experiences of others are early mechanisms of empathy, from an evolutionary and developmental point of view.

Maternal empathy mirrors a powerful mechanism between parents and a child, and there is plenty of behavior to demonstrate that, because a newborn instinctively imitates movements from the first hours after birth. Infants as young as ten weeks spontaneously imitate some rudimentary features of happy and angry expressions displayed by their mothers. At nine months, infants comprehend and mirror the facial expressions of joy and sadness.

In classic attachment theory, the mother tends to be sensitive to her child's needs; mirroring allows her to achieve a powerful affective attunement. The maternal capacity to mirror the infant's internal states may take different forms. It is all based on a neurobiological mechanism. By any means the mother is highly empathic subject when it comes to her baby; her empathy is not as high with other babies, but she can be compassionate.

Humans in general tend to synchronize movements; you fold your arm, I fold my arm; you look back, I look away; you look at me, I look at you. Experiments have indicated that the more people like each other, the more imitation takes place among them. Thus, imitation and synchrony are the glue that binds people together. Therefore, mirror neurons are essential for us to fit ourselves as smoothly as possible into our social context. We are all on the boat of life together, and mirror neurons help us navigate life with less difficulty. We need mirror neurons to help us recognize the actions of other people, imitate other people, and understand their intentions and their feeling.

These phenomena can be very puzzling to neuroscientists; for example, you grasp a cup of coffee, I grasp a cup of coffee. But how does my brain distinguish my action from your action? The most important region in the brain is the *parietal operculum*, in the right cerebral hemisphere, which is the responsible of body awareness. If a patient has some sort of disorder in this region of the brain, they may suffer from lack of awareness of bodily functions. Thus mirror neurons affirm our awareness, and enhance the sense of being the agent of our own actions.

Mirror neurons allow us to understand the emotions of others, and to facilitate social behavior and be a coherent society. We cannot artificially separate the self and others. As Dan Zahavi put it, we are reciprocal illuminations of one another.

We cannot think of being independent of others, because we cannot define ourselves without others, and others cannot define themselves without us. Mirror neurons play a major role here. We are inevitably interdependent. However, neurons fire stronger for the self than for others. Mirror neurons are the glue of society, and it starts when parents imitate a child and a child imitates parents, and this becomes hard wired in our brain.

Self-recognition and imitation go together, because mirror neurons are born when the others imitate the self, early in life. Arguably, mirror neurons are largely shaped by imitative interactions between ourselves and others, especially in the early years of life.

The concept of self is a highly complex one; a host of factors participate in its creation. Charles Darwin conducted experiments on orangutans whereby he put them in front of mirror, and it reflected their image. Although the mirror recognition test became a widely used tool in animal cognition research, the orangutans fail the test. They see their reflection as another orangutan, and try to play with him. When this fails, they look behind the mirror to try to find out what is going on. Animals raised in a human environment pass the experiment. Thus, the social context is critical in developing self-recognition abilities in apes. Moreover, isolation seems to inhibit the ability to develop self-recognition, and a rich social context facilitates it.

What is the difference between the two environments? The presence of others, the continuous relations and interactions one must have with other individuals makes the difference. Because mirror neurons fire when we observe actions and when we perform those same actions, the link between social environment and sense of self is very strong. That self-recognition shows in animals' link between imitation, empathy, and sense of self. Self-recognition in children clearly shows when the child is embarrassed. Embarrassment requires some rudimentary sense of social norms, which are derived from daily interaction with other people.

Some mirror neurons are functioning very early in life and facilitate the earliest interactions. Most of our mirror neuron system is formed during months and years of such interactions. The shaping of mirror neurons in a baby's brain has to happen between the child and the parents or caregiver.

<u>Imitation and autism</u>. All autism research since 1950 indicates there is a deficit in imitation. Non-autistic children understand the beliefs and desires of other people because they have an innate module in their brain that helps them construct theories about other people. Children's inability to resonate emotionally with other people can also be a factor in autism.

The most critically impaired faculty in autism is the social-affective form of imitation, more than the cognitive form. The critical impairment in patients with autism is social mirroring, which is supported by neural interaction between mirror neurons and the limbic system through the insula. Groups of scientists working independently suggested that autism may indeed be associated with a dysfunction in the mirror neuron system (Justin Williams, Andrew Whiten, Dave Parrett). This Scottish team hypothesized there is an early development impairment leading to autism. If this is the case, they believed the key neural deficit in autism was the dysfunction of mirror neurons.

If we go further and research super mirror neurons and their influence on our thinking, we can see how our thinking of a certain subject can have a drastic effect on our intelligence. For example, in a series of experiments, one group of participants was asked to think about college professors, who are typically associated with intelligence, and write down everything that came to mind. A second group was asked to do the same regarding soccer hooligans, those unruly and destructive fans who are typically associated with stupidity.

Then both groups were asked a series of general knowledge questions, unrelated to the first exercise. But it turned out that there was a relationship; the participants who had concentrated earlier on college professors outperformed the participants who had been thinking about soccer hooligans. Indeed, the college professor participants outperformed a control group that came fresh to the general knowledge questions, and this control group in turn outperformed the soccer hooligan participants.

The conclusion: just merely thinking about college professors makes you smarter, whereby thinking about soccer hooligans makes you dumber. As Dijksterhuis summarized in his research, imitation can make us slow, fast, smart, stupid, good at math, bad at math, helpful, rude, polite, long-winded, hostile, aggressive, cooperative, competitive, conforming, nonconforming, conservative, forgetful, careful, careless, neat, or sloppy.

Because constant automatic mimicry is indeed an expression of some form of neural mirroring, such imitation can have fairly complex and subtle behaviors, encompassing cells whose role is controlling and modulation of more classical and simpler mirror neurons. This higher order of mirror neurons is called super mirror neurons. If we map the brain we find the regions of mirror neurons shared by three areas of the frontal lobe: the orbital-frontal cortex, anterior cingulate cortex, and pre-supplementary motor area.

In Arab culture, since we imitate each other's behaviors or attitudes, often the dominant attitudes are oppression or abuse of each other. Our higher mirror neurons fire as we see and identify with each other, and in this case, the result of such mirror neurons is stupidity, or lack of creativity, or abuse of each other. That is not confined to the Arab culture, however, and may be more so with other oppressive cultures around the world.

Further, there is imitative violence, which imitates the violence seen through the media. Exposure to this violence can lead to imitation; mirror neurons could be part of the problem. There is myriad research that shows when we expose children or adults to violence, they tend to imitate the behavior, and that is mirror neurons. A longitudinal study on American children has provided very impressive empirical results in supporting the hypothesis that media violence induces imitative violence.

Where is the free-will of our behavior? Many long-cherished notions about human autonomy are clearly threatened by the neuron scientific scrutiny of the biological roots of human behavior. Our notion of free will can be challenged diabolically; the more we learn about mirror neurons, the more we realize that we are not rational, free-acting agents in the world. Mirror neurons in our brains produce automatic imitative influences of which we are often unaware, and that limit our autonomy by means of powerful social influences (*Mirror Neurons*, by Marco Iacoboni).

Humans are social animals, yet our society makes us social agents with limited autonomy. The observation of violence can cause arousal; that may facilitate imitative violence, by reducing the inhibitory activities of super neurons. We may think of ourselves as autonomous people, but in reality mirror neurons make us like a monkey; monkey see, monkey do. Our instinct for empathy, however, is part of the good news stemming from mirror neurons.

There is a close relationship between mirror neurons and addiction, or relapse. For example, when a former smoker watches other people smoking, mirror neurons are automatically activated.

Are we really independent of other people's opinions? For example, if you sit with a group of people, the social pressure to say the proper thing often overwhelms true opinion, and that is due to the power of imitation in human interactions; it is human nature to be part of the crowd. In Arab society, once you veer from social norms, you are an outcast and ostracized. This is not so common in Western society, but it is very common in collectivist societies where the tribe, or the dogma of religions dominates over the masses. The dire consequences can be deprivation, or stripping of individual freedom, or lack of creativity, which makes the whole society docile, and sheep easy to be led. Painfully, that is the condition of the Arab people at present.

We like to think of ourselves as autonomous agents, in control of our own lives and able to make decisions in a rational and conscious way. However, there is plenty of evidence to suggest this is not necessarily the case. Much psychological research has shown that our ability to make decisions and having our own original experiences is really limited. Sometimes we are not aware of our own choices. There are so many factors influencing our decisions and choices. Mirror neurons play a major role in that which makes us automatically internalize other people's behavior. And that can jeopardize free will.

Chapter Twelve

If You Resist, It Will Persist: The Nature of the Sly Mind

How can we control unwanted thoughts? The harder you try to stop thinking about something, the harder it is to let go. The more effort you put into avoiding that thought, the faster it pops back up in your consciousness.

Harvard psychologist Daniel Wegner, in his book *Mental Control*, showed that trying very hard not to think about something almost guarantees that we will think about it. It seems paradoxical, but it makes sense. When you are actively avoiding a thought, one part of your brain is busy working to keep the upsetting thought at bay. At the same time, another part of the mental machinery keeps checking to make sure that the job is being done properly.

The best illustration of this condition is, if a baby is sleeping, the mother wants to make sure the baby is asleep and all right, so she keeps checking him by touching him to make sure that he is sleeping. By touching him she is waking him up. That is exactly what the mind is doing with thoughts. Once you want a thought to leave your mind, the thought keeps staying, and will not leave you.

Inadvertently, this monitoring process calls attention to the unwanted thought, and makes you more vulnerable to the very ideas you are fleeing from. The funny thing is, when you are trying not to think about something, you have to remember what it is you are not thinking about. That memory, that part of your mind which is trying to keep it fresh, is going to activate thought. It is a paradoxical process.

It is a lot like trying to fall sleep, or forcing yourself to relax. The harder you try, the more likely you will stay wide awake. Struggling for control over the mind only makes it worse; the more we try to control thoughts, the more they do what they want. In seemingly paradoxical therapy, you do the opposite of the thing you want to do, and perhaps that is the cure.

In a case from my private practice a few years ago in Michigan, a patient came to see me and said she has had trouble sleeping for few months and nothing was working for her. I picked up a thick book, and asked her to read and summarize it within two nights, and I asked her not to sleep. She came to me after a couple of days and said as soon as she opened the book, she fell asleep. "I do not know what's so special about this book, but it literally paralyzed me and I cannot keep myself awake." I said, "this is exactly what happens to you when you do not focus on something, that thing tends to come. When you suspended the thought of sleep, sleep came to you."

Thoughts endeavor to resist you vehemently when you try to eject them from your mind. Ousting unwanted thoughts from your mind, or vacating your mind from disturbing thoughts can be an overwhelming task, but if you persist, eventually the thought will perish. To overcome negative thoughts, and replace with positive ones, remember, courage overcomes fears, patience overcomes anger and irritability, love overcomes hatred. You also have to be persistent in your spiritual practice. If you are tenacious and diligent, you are bound to succeed.

The law of resistance. Carl Jung came up with the concept of resistance. Whenever we experience discontentment or are unhappy, there is inevitably something we are resisting. All suffering is caused by non-acceptance of a thought or a feeling, an emotion or a situation. You suffer when you want things to be different from what they are. Unfortunately, what you resist, persists. Often, it is not the experience itself that causes pain and suffering, but rather the resistance to the experience. How we label the experience determines how we feel about it.

From a young age, we are conditioned to categorize our experiences into good and bad, right and wrong, desirable and undesirable. For example, if you feel down, the mind unconsciously labels the feeling as bad. There is nothing wrong with feeling sad, unless the mind says so, and it produces statements about what is wrong with us. If you say yes to the experience, you will not suffer and will have inner peace. If you resist the experience, it will persist. This is the law of attraction.

Whatever you are trying to fight against will continue to be present. Albert Einstein said "energy never gets destroyed, it can only change form", so you cannot just delete parts of the universe, you can only change it into something else. To put in terms as a law, if you resist something, its only option is to carry on as it is, until it is given the option to do something else. For example, if you keep telling your friend, do not eat large portions of food, they will keep eating, even if there are dire consequences. Until there is an alternative way to eat different or healthy food, and you are no longer resisting, you are moving in the other direction.

What you resist not only persists, but will grow according to Jung. Society has taught us that to get rid of whatever it is we do not want. We must never show weakness and never lose focus. This thought and belief has been responsible for much damage and has caused much pain to individuals and societies. The best example of preaching to people, do not do that, but do this, is in the Arab world. Eventually, people tire of hearing preachers all their lives, became numb, and do not pay attention. Often, they do the opposite of what they hear. In the Arab world, preaching has paralyzed the mind of the people and given them a bad taste about the message and the preachers.

A far better and more peaceful approach is to consciously offer no resistance, as what you embrace dissolves. Negative states persist because we give them energy and importance, through giving them all of our attention. When we offer no resistance, they wither and fade away, and you have a sense of peace.

When you focus your thoughts on one specific thing, it is that thing you will attract to yourself, whether it is what you want or not. When you start to think of something you also set in motion the vibrations that will attract whatever it is on which you are focused to you. By consciously thinking about what it is you do not want, you have given it strength. You have developed that neural pathway into a highway, a highway that will keep bringing you the same type of person or events.

Deepak Chopra said that when you engage in an inner war between what you crave and what you know is good for you, defeat is all but inevitable. In its natural state, will is the opposite of resistance. What we resist only serves to draw more of the same to us. Through focusing on what we do not want, we attract more of it. For example, worrying is like praying for that which we do not want.

Whatever you fight, you strengthen, and what you resist, persists (Eckhart Tolle.) No amount of strength will change that we are human, and do not need to suffer endlessly. Thus, stop fighting natural duality. There is no reason to pretend you are smiling when you are crying silently inside. Nature needs to follow its course, and the moment we decide to swim against the current, to make things suit our selfish needs, we cannot expect not to pay the consequences. Thus, we have to accept what life offers, or we are like a rigid tree in the midst of a storm. If we keep on living that way, we will eventually break down. If we choose to be flexible and "go with the flow", nothing bad will ever happen to us.

Resistance and physical pain. The conflict with pain hinders our growth as a spiritual being. Resistance is a creating energy; it reinforces the very pain you are trying to avoid, giving it strength to continue in your life. We resist life on a daily basis, being impatient, stubborn, late, arrogant and procrastinate, to name just a few. Anger and smoking are also forms of resistance as well.

How to stop, and do what works? It is rather similar to smoking. It is so difficult to stop smoking, because people try to stop. This is may seem a bit backward, but this apparently nonsensical statement highlights the problem. Many people stop at least a dozen times. We have to stop doing what does not work. When you try to stop smoking you are ignoring this significant law of the universe.

It's obvious that energy is creative. If you put your energy into what you do not want, then you are energizing what you do not want. Despite the negative, what you do not want get stronger, because you are giving it energy, and so it persists. When you attempt to stop smoking, you are giving energy to not smoking, meaning you are ignoring the natural law. In trying to resist smoking, you are energizing smoking, so smoking persists.

Instead, focus positively on what you want, which is a healthy lifestyle or vibrant good health. The key principle is: being against something will only bring you more of it. As Jesus Christ said, resist no evil. What does that mean? It means evil force awakes by resisting it. We need to become conscious of what we are manifesting in life; when we wake up, we start to recognize just what we are choosing to energize. For most of us it comes as a surprise to realize that we are actually choosing to energize what comes to us. We tend to go through life on "automatic pilot," but once we realize what we do to ourselves, through various ways of self-sabotage, we require conscious effort to watch our thoughts. Resist no evil also means ignore what is not desirable; turn away, do not even look at it.

Whatever uncomfortable things repeat themselves in your life, shows where you are, neurotically resisting desirable personal growth. When you resist things you tend to be unhappy. But do you want to be right, or do you want to be happy? Often resistance pushes you to be right. In summation, we need our resistance, even our neurotic ones. But to maximize our happiness and potential, we need to weed out neurotic ones, one by one, by changing our emotions, thinking, and spiritual tendencies.

Chapter Thirteen

Culture and Mass Delusions

Albert Einstein said reality is merely an illusion, albeit a very persistent one.

Our mind plays tricks on us and robs our happiness. Our mind is complex and is often our own worst enemy. When it comes to being happy, our mind deceives us into thinking something is right, when it is really wrong, or that we are in love when we are not. Society is a collection of people, and since the mind is deceiving us most of the time, we collectively manifest some delusional thoughts. As Fredrick Nietzsche said, pathology is rare in an individual, while it is common in societies.

How the culture shapes our perceptions. David Eagleman indicated that culture leaves its signature in the circuitry of the individual brain. If you were to examine a corn kernel, it could tell you a great deal about its surroundings, from moisture to microbes to the sunlight conditions of the field and forest. By analogy, an individual brain reflects its culture. Our opinions on normality, customs, dress codes, and local superstitions are absorbed into our neural circuitry from the "social forest" around us.

To a surprising extent, one can have a glimpse of a culture by studying a brain. For example, moral attitudes toward cows, pigs, crosses and burkas can be read from the physiological response of the brain in different cultures. Our unconscious mind can be in the driver's seat and influence us, both from the inside (genetics) and outside (society), causing cognitive illusion. For example, visual illusion reveals perceptions generated by the brain do not necessarily correlate with reality. Hallucinations, dreams, and delusions all illustrate this point.

We do not have a strong grip of what reality is out there; we can only detect a small slice of it. Therefore, our brain projects its own materials on the reality, and we tend to believe it, but if we examine it closely, we are really far from real reality. There is no consented agreement over reality, because every one of us has a different reality. Even twin brothers, if you ask them, each has a different reality.

Parents and cultures often instill in us all kinds of things since childhood, and these values are coded in our neurons whether we like it or not. As adults, we have to behave according to cultural roles and practices. Thus, culture can shape our pattern of thoughts, and we carry on the practices helplessly.

Daniel Hahnemann said focusing illusions, how people think, usually is somewhat more conscious than a lower-level cognitive process such as perceptions. We are not at all aware of the process by which we recognize a cat when we see one; we are not aware when we retrieve a word for a conversation. But we are aware when we resolve math problems.

If delusions are accepted by the masses they become a belief. Delusion is a belief that is sustained, despite what almost everyone else believes, and is not ordinarily accepted by other members of the person's culture or subculture. Since we live in a delusional society, that is becoming the norm. That makes this type of thinking non-delusional, because everybody else thinks the same. Thus, delusions are false judgments, held with extraordinary conviction and subjective certainty, resistant to contrary experiences and counter argument, whose content is impossible, or at least not verifiable.

The human mind is characterized by two antagonistic forces struggling for supremacy, intellect and instinct, each trying to achieve dominance. In some situations the instinctive forces gain control in a way to encourage individuals involved in a group, mass or mob. Here the herd instinct becomes supreme, with the inclination to organize, follow, and obey a leader. The causes of such mass delusion are conformity, pluralistic ignorance, illusion of unanimity and illusion of invulnerability.

Friedrich Nietzsche said insanity in individuals is something rare, but in a group, party, nation or epoch, it is the rule. Insanity or delusions in groups exist because whatever is most popular in the group is selected as a replacement for reality itself. This occurs in part because a more easily comprehended idea will be more popular, and in part because people prefer to believe what they want to be true, not what is true.

But there is another mechanism that is more insidious. It has two parts, positive and negative, and the group determines what succeeds. The positive part of this mechanism is if you want to succeed in society, you need to come up with something that is popular. Then people buy it, vote for it, and demand it in social circles. For example, in the French Revolution, if you did not cheer enough when they beheaded someone, you were seen as a possible enemy of the state. It can make you the next person at the guillotine. The execution of ideological enemies unites a group to such a degree that turning on itself is a net win. Welcome to being a cog in the machine of society, which can strip you of your humanity.

Lawrie Reznek, in 2010, wrote a book about mass delusion. He indicated many of us tend to cling to beliefs that provide comfort, meaning, and bolster our self-esteem. Further, normal people acquire beliefs through irrational biases such as the illusory correlation error. Delusions, whether secular or religious, are dangerous because they are false things that matter to people who hold them with conviction. He also said the whole world is mad, with irrationality pervasive throughout normal people. The failure of reason seems to characterize normality, and no person seems free of delusional ideas. We all seem to have succumbed to the sleep of reason, spawning delusional ideas and making monsters of us all.

Delusion can increase violence in society by creating rumors about any individual or institution or political party, and people accept it wholesale, without examination. If you challenge such societal beliefs, you become an outcast, shunned by the majority. This is how wars start. Often, the machine of the government dehumanizes others, and people go to war to fight people they do not know and with whom they have never even had a slight encounter. The most ridiculous and stupid thing people even consider is that a war is a holy act, and sacrifice their souls, because of the indoctrination of mass delusion.

Dictators throughout history have benefitted greatly from the mass delusion of society. The machine of the dictators spread rumors of how he is God's gift to humanity, and that is repeated through the media. Soon the false propaganda will become a reality for the people and becomes for them a core belief. The human mind is very vulnerable to mass suggestion. Once the media repeats them over and over, it becomes a subliminal message and enters the unconscious mind of people, and becomes part of their collective reality.

As far as mass delusion, we need to mention identification with aggressors, which is another face for mass delusion. People in general are weak and fearful, so when someone comes and threatens their survival, they have to find a means to ensure it, by implementing the best defense from the menace of the aggressor. That is to identify with the aggressor, and become part of his machine of oppression. If the aggressor is faced with a threat, they will not hesitate to defend him by any means.

A psychological merger between the aggressor and the abused individuals takes place. History is filled with this dynamic of mass delusion. In Iraq or Syria it reached the stage that a son killed his father or a father killed his son, after merely being asked by the aggressor to do so. Fear of the aggressor overwhelms the whole being of the individual, and their survival supersedes anything else.

In general, people do not like to examine things around them, because that requires a lot of mental energy and mental awareness, and people do not want that. They choose the easy way, which is acceptance without examination. Most societies are loaded with delusional thinking, and it becomes the repertoire of the society. The human mind is lazy and does not want to go the extra mile to verify or sift out myth from reality. Therefore, we will always have the herd mentality, and mass delusions, because people want to be part of the crowd. Rarely, you find an individual who stands alone, immune from other opinions. Those individuals are the reformers who enrich the human community with their own unique contributions. Since we have this part of human fallibility, there will always be a place for mass delusion and dictatorship.

Chapter Fourteen

Left Brain vs. Right Brain

Research on brain theory helps us understand why some people are inventors, while other people poor producers, or a good manager, or a weak leader. Research also indicates the brain is divided into two hemispheres, each one specializing in different functions, and dealing with different kinds of problems. The left brain works more with logic and analysis, and the right brain works more with emotion and imagination.

Mental ability, or intelligence, is an aggregate of many special abilities, of which problem solving is only one. Many studies have shown that men excel in information subjects such as history and science, while women are superior in reading, language, spelling, and math.

You may have heard of people describing themselves as strictly right-brained or left-brained, with the left-brained bragging about their math skills and the right-brained touting their creativity. Because the brain is divided into two hemispheres with each half performing a distinctive set of operations, both of them operate independently as well as in concert with each other. The two communicate information, such as sensory observations, to each other through the thick corpus callosum that connects them.

The right brain controls the muscles on the left side of the body, and the left brain controls the muscles of the right side of the body. When you wink your right eye, that is the left side of your brain at work. Because of this cross-wiring, damage to one side of the brain affects the opposite side of the body.

In general, the left hemisphere is dominant in language processing, what you hear, and handling most of speech. It also handles logic and exact mathematical computation. When you want to retrieve a fact, your left brain pulls it from your memory. The right hemisphere is mainly in charge of spatial abilities, face recognition, and processing music. It performs some math, but only rough estimations. The right brain helps us to comprehend visual imagery and make sense of what we see. It plays some roles in language, particularly in interpreting context and personal tone.

Whether a person is right-brained or left-brained, the performance of the two sections are far more complex than just a simple left vs. right equation. The brain is carefully balanced, and assigns control of certain functions to each side. It is all nature's way of ensuring that the brain ultimately splits any tasks to maximize efficiency. Most people are right-hand dominant, controlled by the left side of the brain.

Brain asymmetry is essential for proper brain function. People who identify as left-brained thinkers might feel that they have strong math and logic skills. Those who profess to be right-brained, on the other hand, feel talented, and are on the creative side. People say that they prefer one type of thinking over the other; for example, a person who is left-brained is often to be more logical, analytical, intuitive, thoughtful, and subjective.

This theory of lateralization of brain function originated in the work of Roger W. Sperry, who was awarded the Nobel Prize in 1981, while he was studying the effects of epilepsy. Sperry postulated that disconnecting or cutting the corpus callosum could reduce or eliminate seizures.

Neuroscientists today believe the two sides of the brain collaborate to perform a broad variety of tasks and the two hemispheres communicate through the corpus callosum. For example, the left hemisphere specializes in picking out the sounds that form words and working out the syntax of the phrase, but it does not have a monopoly on language processing. The right hemisphere is more sensitive to the emotional features of language.

A University of Utah study analyzed the brains of more than 1,000 people to determine if they preferred using one side over the other. The study revealed that while activity was sometimes higher in certain regions, both sides of the brain were essentially equal in their activity. Right-brained dominance theory is associated with the following functions: recognizing faces, expressing emotion, reading music, color, images, intuition, and creativity. Left-brained dominance considers the following functions: language, logic, critical thinking, numbers and reasoning. This theory is probably outdated, but is still in use.

The theory of brain dominance has prevailed for several years; too bad it's not true. New research conducted by the University of Utah scanned the brains of more than 1,000 people while they were lying quietly or reading.

Functional lateralization, the specific mental process taking place in each side of human brain, was measured. They broke the brain into 7,000 regions, and while they did uncover patterns for why a brain connection might be strongly left or right lateralization, they found no evidence that the study participants had a strong left or right sided brain network.

Jeff Anderson, the study's leading author, says, "it is absolutely true that some brain functions occur in one or the other side of the brain." Language tends to be on the left, attention more on the right, but the brain is not as clear cut as we may profess.

What research has yet to refute is that the brain is remarkably malleable, even into late adulthood. It has an amazing ability to reorganize itself by forming new connections between brain cells, allowing us to continually learn new things and modify our behavior. Let us not underestimate our potential by allowing a simplistic myth to obscure the complexity of how the brain really works. Sometimes ideas that originate in science seep out into the broader culture and take on a life of their own.

There are a few myths about the functions of the brain. The first myth is that we use only 10% of our brain, and if we can do all the things we do using 10% of our brain, just imagine what we could accomplish if we used the remaining 90%. That is the popular belief. However, research suggests that all areas of the brain perform some type of function. If the 10% myth was true, brain damage would be far less likely. We would really only have to worry about that tiny 10% of our brain being injured. Brain imaging technologies have also demonstrated that the entire brain shows levels of activity, even during sleep. The brain is active all the time, all parts. The brain represents three percent of body weight, and uses 20% of the body's energy.

A second myth: brain damage is permanent. The brain is fragile and can be damaged by things such as injury, stroke, or disease. This damage can result in a range of consequences from mild disruption in cognitive abilities to complete impairment. Brain damage can be devastating, but it depends on the severity and location of the injury. For example, a blow to the head during a football game might lead to concussion. While this can be quite serious, most people are able to recover when given time to heal. A severe stroke, on the other hand, can result in dire consequences and can be permanent.

It is important to remember that the human brain has an impressive amount of plasticity. Even following a serious brain event such as a stroke, the brain can heal itself over time and form new connections. Research indicates the brain may be capable of developing new connections, and rerouting functions through healthy areas.

The third myth: people are either right- or left-brained. It is a popular notion that we are dominated either by the right or left brain hemisphere. The reality is, there is lateralization of brain function, with certain types of tasks and thinking more associated with a particular region of the brain. But no one is fully right- or left-brained. In fact, we tend to do better at tasks when the entire brain is utilized, even for things that are typically associated with certain areas of the brain. No matter how lateralized the brain can get, the two sides still work together.

The fourth myth: humans have the biggest brain. The human brain is quite large in proportion to body size, but there is a common misconception is that humans have the largest brain of any organism. The average adult has a brain weighing about three pounds and measuring up to 15 centimeters in length. The sperm whale brain weighs 18 pounds, and another large-brained animal is the elephant, whose brain weighs 11 pounds.

The fifth myth: we are born with all the brain cells we ever have, and once they die, these cells are gone forever. Traditional wisdom has long suggested that adults only have so many brain cells, and once these cells are lost, they are gone for good. New research has discovered evidence that the human adult brain does indeed form new cells through life, even during old age. The process of forming new brain cells is known as neurogenesis and researchers have found that it happens in at least in one important region of the brain called the hippocampus (Dan Cassin).

The sixth myth: drinking alcohol kills brain cells. Some people might warn you that you will lose precious brain cells that you never get back with excessive or chronic alcohol abuse. It can certainly have dire health consequences, but scientific medical research has actually demonstrated that moderate consumption of alcohol is associated with better cognition (thinking and reasoning) skills and memory, than is abstaining from alcohol. Moderate drinking does not kill brain cells, but helps the brain function better into old age. Studies around the world involving many thousands of people report this finding (PsychCentral.Com).

The seventh myth: There are 100 billion neurons in the human brain. In 2009, one researcher decided to actually count neurons in the adult brain and found that the number was a bit off the mark. Based upon this research, it appears that the human brain contains closer to 85 billion neurons. Still, 85 billion is nothing to sneeze at. People are still hung up on 100 billion, though.

As with physical exercise, working on both sides of the brain enables them to sharpen and coordinate. Individuals should not reject brain exercise due to age or background, according to neuroscientist Dr. Marian C. Diamond at the University of California-Berkeley. Diamond maintained that the process of learning at any stage of life stimulates nerve cells to form dendrites linking knowledge and experiences, and forming what she calls the hardware of intelligence.

There are numerous exercises to sharpen the brain. Visualization, games like chess or checkers, the stoop test, or everyday strategies that change your tendencies toward everyday problem-solving, keep both sides of the brain active. Instead of defining issues or creating strategies, a right brain function, try approaching a problem spontaneously and instinctively. Alternatively, curb your impulsiveness and focus on practical, or reality-based solutions.

Keep in mind that individuals who are more left-brain dominant may adapt to a new environment before learning its specific demands or requirements. By comparison, people who are right-brain dominant may be so focused on deadlines, rules or regulations that they may be unable to appreciate the large significance of an event. However, brain exercise should not be considered a substitute for a healthy lifestyle, which includes making sensible choices for eating and exercising regularly. Besides exercising the brain, it is also essential to feed the brain with the right food; the last chapter of this book discusses that.

Chapter Fifteen

The Power of Suggestion

What is suggestion? It is a tendency in human nature to believe any statement that is repeated a great number of times. This tendency to believe has nothing to do with the truth of the statement. Reasons for believing that statement to be true or false are not taken into account; the statement is believed solely because it is repeated many times. There are many explanation for human suggestibility, none of which is entirely satisfactory. Everyone is suggestible but it varies, to pinch an idea from George Orwell's *Animal Farm*. Successful advertisers and propagandists understand this very well. There is no power so persuasive as the power of suggestion. The first fact to note about suggestion is, statements rely on suggestion.

The suggestive statement must be simply expressed, with confidence in tone, and repeated often, if we want it to be accepted or effective. A single halting statement is not persuasive. A confident statement, often repeated, is immensely persuasive. Simplicity in expression gives the statement a better chance for acceptance than complexity. That's what advertisements rely on; they state the message as a slogan, which gives it an air of confidence. If we keep repeating the statement over and over, it goes to our unconscious mind and we behave accordingly, or we can develop our biases and prejudices.

The subtle psychological power of suggestion. Most of our beliefs are held not because we have verified them for ourselves but for many other different reasons. Some of these reasons range from the influence of environment in childhood to the influence of the media in adult life. They all have one factor in common: their appeal to and effect upon human suggestibility. Humans in general are susceptible to suggestion, and this is of enormous importance, both in our individual lives and in the life of the society in which we live.

The role of individual difference. Given the variety of instances in which suggestion can have an impact on our lives and behavior, its fair to propose that our vulnerability to suggestion might be all too common a part of what it is to be human. Gaddis (2004) indicated that the first impulse of people is to believe. Doubting is usually secondary and the power of suggestion wields a tremendous influence on our lives and opinions. There is a considerable amount of research regarding individual suggestibility. For example, the intelligent person who is able to manipulate an interrogation situation when there is a conflict with the law, or a highly acquiescent individual are more open to suggestion, as are people with low self-esteem, seen as low effectiveness of achievement. All these types of people are susceptible to suggestion, because they doubt their own opinions of themselves (Dr. Krissy Wilson).

The effects of suggestion play a much larger role in shaping our lives than most of us realize. When we expect a specific outcome, we automatically set in motion a chain of cognitions and behavior to produce that outcome, and wrongly attribute our success or failure to its cause. Maryanne Garry and Robert Michael of Victoria University in Wellington, New Zealand, along with Irving Kirsch of Harvard Medical School, investigated the phenomenon of suggestion. They explored the relationship between suggestion, cognition, and behavior. They found that our response expectations are influenced by our prior experiences, our present beliefs, and the situations in which we find ourselves.

We encounter suggestion every day of our lives. We like to believe that our thoughts and behavior are rationally constructed, but research shows it is not only deliberate suggestion that influences our thoughts and behaviors, but suggestions that are not deliberate can have the same effect. Simply observing people or otherwise making them feel special can be suggestion, and such a phenomenon can be attributed to the Hawthorne Effect.

The Hawthorne Effect refers to the tendency of some people to work and perform better when they are a participant in an experiment. Individuals may change their behavior due to the attention they are receiving from researchers, rather than manipulation of independent variables. Or it can be the observer effect, a type of reactivity in which the individual modifies or improves an aspect of their behavior in response to their awareness of being observed. It is a psychological phenomenon that produces an improvement in human behavior or performance as a result of increased attention from people around them. The effect operates like peer pressure, to improve the behavior of a participant, or it can be defined as the effect of expectation, which has been seen in a wide range of situations.

An entire industry has risen from the idea that through the power of suggestion we can change and improve our lives. Books, magazines and TV programs all offer ways in which self-hypnosis and the power of positive thought can help us to give up smoking, lose weight, be more assertive, bolster our career and improve our life.

The effectiveness of suggestion has been demonstrated over and over in every field, from medicine to human behavior. The notion of suggestibility is of interest to psychologists from all corners of the discipline, as it encompasses a wide variety of areas relating to cognitive, social and personality factors. Is suggestibility a personality trait, cognitive bias, distortion of memory, or all of these elements?

Most research has looked at the nature of suggestion on the impact of memory. Elizabeth Lotus (1979), demonstrated how a leading question and suggestive information can seriously distort a person's memory of an observed event. The pernicious effect of suggestive procedure has also been explored in relation to the creation of false memory within therapy. Years of empirical research suggest that false memories of childhood sexual abuse, reports of alien abduction and vivid tales of past lives, may share a similarity with fantasy-based memories, as a response to hypnotic or other suggestive procedures.

Suggestive techniques have been examined critically in the forensic setting, since the suggestion depends on the biases of the interrogator. That leads to contamination of the memory of an individual. The best example is Paul Ingram (Wright, 1994), when his daughter accused him of child abuse. The police throughout the interrogation told him he must has committed the crime. He finally gave a false story and admitted to the bizarre crime. He fabricated the whole thing, because of the power of suggestion by the police. Eventually, with the help of psychologist Richard Ofshe, he left jail, as he had never committed the crime in the first place.

Why some people miraculously get better when given a placebo has baffled us for years. However, scientists have now linked the mysterious phenomenon to genes. Placebos are usually sugar-coated pills given to patients in clinical studies to compare response to the actual drug vs. the placebo. Until now people put the surprise effect down to the power of suggestion. But Tomas

Furmark, of Uppsala University in Sweden, has now linked the placebo effect to people with an exaggerated fear of public humiliation, to the gene for tryptophan hydroxylase-2, which makes the brain chemical serotonin.

In another study, 25 people who suffer from social anxiety disorder challenged their fear by giving two speeches, before and after a treatment period of eight weeks. Participants believed they were given an active drug when they actually received a placebo. Ten people responded to the sham treatment, and felt half as anxious during the second speech, while the others were just as nervous. Brain scans also showed 3% lower activity in the amygdala, the fear center in the brain.

A placebo is the power of suggestion; the physician suggests to the patient that the pills are very effective to cure disease, and the patient takes it to heart, and it has great effect. Believing that something may do you good, often produces positive results. A sizeable minority will show a measurable, observable improvement in their condition, having taken nothing more than an inert placebo.

Charron (2006), showed the power of placebos for patients suffering from back pain, and similar results have been shown as well with response to irritable bowel syndrome. Kirsch and Sapirstein, in the meta-analysis of some 39 studies on the effectiveness of Prozac with patients who suffer from depression, concluded that placebos could account for more than 50% of patients' improvement, and the rest to Prozac. Another study conducted by the Scottish Institutes of Sport found that a placebo can improve athletic performance the same as taking steroids.

Suggestion is evident in magic. Magicians have explored our vulnerability to suggestion for centuries in order to achieve all kinds of illusions and sleight of hand tricks. For example, when verbal suggestion succeeds in diverting the attention of an audience, the magician removes the object on which the "magic trick" is based. It is much easier to fool a room full of scientists than a classroom of children, since the scientist looks for cause and effect, whereas children rely on observations. Suggestion and the paranormal are fascinating phenomena. However, skeptics have pointed to suggestion as trickery and chicanery involved in the demonstration of alleged paranormal abilities by psychics and mediums.

Suggestion means you get what you expect to get. Thus, expectation is the key. Science has found the genie emerges from the bottle when our expectation of success mobilizes vast cognitive and emotional resources and directs those resources toward fulfilling our desire. In other words, we get what we expect to get. This phenomenon, again, is called the placebo effect, the power of suggestion

The landmark research of Ellen Langer of Harvard showed the power of suggestion could roll back the biological clock by 20 years for men in their late 70s and early 80s. She also found it can increase eyesight by 40%, and allow you to lose weight at a rapid rate. The power of suggestion can improve cognitive function, reduce pain, and even change the outcome in a deadly disease such as non-Hodgkins lymphoma. The proof is there; the power of suggestion can shape our reality, mainly when the power of suggestion is fused with expectation. The odds go up that you will get what you are hoping to get. It modifies, the old proverb, "be careful what you ask for".

Hypnotic suggestion. Operationally, hypnosis refers to a change in baseline mental activity after an induction procedure, and is typically experienced at the subjective level as an increase in absorption and focused attention to extraneous stimuli and a reduction in spontaneous thought. Hypnotic induction procedures facilitate this particular mental state. Typical hypnotic phenomena such as alteration in sensory experience and motor control, amnesia and adoption of false beliefs about the self and environment, require specific suggestion. There is good evidence that a subject can respond to a suggestion of this sort within the need to employ formal induction procedure.

Indeed, the best predictor of the suggestibility of an individual in hypnosis is their responsiveness to the same suggestion outside hypnosis. The effect of hypnotic suggestion can be more evident at the level of brain activation and it has been shown that the same suggestion can be used to increase or decrease fibromyalgia pain. The second important distinction within hypnosis research concerns the attempt to elucidate the neuron-cognitive nature of hypnosis with studies that use hypnotic suggestion as a means for exploring a range of psychological phenomena such as memory, perception, pain, hallucination or voluntary control of action.

There have been some notable attempts to draw together neuropsychological and phenomenological evidence for hypnosis as an altered state of consciousness, with particular emphasis on the roles of the anterior cingulate and dorsolateral frontal cortical areas. Rainville compared a non-hypnosis baseline condition with a hypnosis condition that produced and coordinated a pattern of activity, and they both involved the brainstem, thalamus, anterior cingulate cortex, right inferior frontal gyrus and right inferior parietal lobe. These activations were interpreted as evidence that mental absorption is an experiential correlate of the executive attention network, and central to the production of a hypnotic experience. A study by Q. Deeley showed hypnosis as a means of systematically modulating sustained attention and independent stimulus.

Studies show that hypnosis can treat everything from chronic pain to poor study habits. But can you be hypnotized? Most people like to think they cannot. There is often the suspicion that being hypnotized could label them as being weak-willed, naive or unintelligent. But in fact, modern research shows that hypontizability is correlated with intelligence, concentration, and focus. Hypnosis is not an all-or-nothing phenomenon, but rather a continuum. Most people can be hypnotized to some degree; the only question is how far?

A hypnotic trance is not therapeutic in and of itself, but specific suggestion and images fed to a patient in a trance can profoundly alter their behavior. As they rehearse new ways they want to think and feel, they lay the groundwork for powerful changes in their future actions. For example, if a person wants to stop smoking, he has to go a few hours without a cigarette and they have to maintain the image of themselves as a nonsmoker. Some combination of finding themselves breathing easier, having more energy for exercise, enjoying subtle taste and smells again, having fresh breath and clean-smelling clothes, feeling good about their health, even saving money on cigarettes, motivates that person to quit smoking.

The deep relaxation of a hypnotic trance is also broadly beneficial for many illnesses, both psychological and physical, which are aggravated by anxiety and muscle tension. Research over the last 40 years shows that such hypnotic techniques are safe and effective. Furthermore, a growing number of studies show that hypnotherapy can treat headache, ease the pain of childbirth, aid in quitting smoking, improve concentration and study habits, relieve minor phobias, and serve as anesthesia, all without drugs or side effects (*Hypnotic Healing*).

We are also learning that both biological and environmental factors predict how deeply a person goes into a trance. Identical twins reared apart often have strikingly similar responses to hypnosis. Dr. Herbert Spiegel, implies that hypnosis has a neurological underpinning, suggesting anesthesia could blunt cortical activities in areas of the brain associated with pain, while asking hypnotized people to hallucinate an image could produce activity in the visual cortex. Early experience also plays a role. Children who are encouraged to engage in imaginative play and creative activities, for instance, usually grow up to respond strongly to hypnosis.

It is also becoming clear the skills one needs to respond to hypnosis are similar to those necessary to experience trance-like states in daily life. The best predictors are a propensity to become absorbed in fantasy imagery and a knack for blocking out the surrounding world. Research suggests the two groups of people who are most easily hypnotized are fantasizers and dissociates. But these groups are only 5% of the general population.

Fantasizers in early life develop great memories, and their recollections are highly detailed. Their memories have been unusual since an early age. If a child was abused, he or she tends to resort to fantasy or imaginary companions to restore self-esteem. Fantasizers have lively imaginations, and visual images can trigger physical sensations. They describe feeling hot and wanting a cool drink in response to seeing photos of a desert. They also shiver through snowy scenes. In another study, half of female fantasizers have experienced false pregnancy at some point in their lives, complete with physiological changes.

Many fantasizers even reach orgasm through imagination alone. They do so by conjuring up scenarios both vivid and varied, involving partners of both sexes. Hypnosis is a natural extension of all these whimsical experiences. Most fantasizers find being in a formal trance more vivid than other imagery in their lives. And they do not remember anything about hypnosis after exiting a trance.

Dissociates experience a separate state of consciousness during hypnosis. Those subjects reported a history of child abuse. Some remembered it directly, others were told they had been battered, and one suspected it. Other children suffered childhood trauma, such as a prolonged painful medical condition before age 10, or the death of parents. Some developed the ability not to think about unpleasant things. They grow these skills to use subconsciously. They may become reliant on them in the face of abuse or trauma.

While fantasizers have an excellent recall for daydreaming and stories that captured their imagination, dissociates are usually unable to recall them. Somewhat like fantasizers, dissociates report that images in their daily lives can produce physical sensations, most of which are negative. They also can be disturbed by even mild sexual fantasies.

Overall, 95% of people are susceptible to hypnotic suggestion to a varying degree. Whether you use it to relieve stress, stop a headache, or get over bad habits, hypnosis is a tool for better health that practically everyone can use. It will work, but it depends on you.

It has been reported in Lancet (2000), that hypnosis given during surgical radiology not only diminishes the patient's pain and anxiety, it also shortens surgical time and reduces complication from the procedure. In a study of patients who suffer nausea and vomiting not only after chemotherapy, but before, hypnosis alleviated pre-chemotherapy sickness in all of them (*Oncology*, 2000).

Hypnosis seems to significantly raise the activities of B-cells and T-cells; both are key to immune response in a highly hypnotizable subject (*American Journal of Clinical Hypnosis*, 1995). There is also a study conducted by the American Lung Association (2000), where 3000 smokers participated in one group hypnotherapy session. Twenty-two percent of them kicked the habit and did not smoke for months. Another study with children who suffer ADD shows that hypnosis is as effective as Ritalin in treatment, as far as pain control is concerned. And 169 patients involved in self-hypnosis were largely successful in alleviating chronic tension and headache.

In summary, suggestion can be a very powerful tool to change the lives of people, whether in the form of hypnosis, or just simple messages repeated over and over, until they go to the unconscious mind and become part of our beliefs. Clearly, in any culture, people develop their biases or prejudices merely by sharing the message about certain groups most of their lives.

Eventually, the negative message may become part of the fabric of the unconscious mind. At that point prejudices or biases establish deep roots in the unconscious mind, and people start to hate another group, even if they have no encounters with them. However we can also use the power of suggestion positively to change our life. The messages of suggestion can be used on a personal level to enhance our growth and development. Because suggestion is a double-edged sword, depending on how it's used. But, overall it is a great tool.

Chapter Sixteen

The Negative Frame of Mind

Winston Churchill said, "a pessimist sees the difficulty in every opportunity; an optimist sees the opportunity in every difficulty"

Where do automatic negative thoughts come from? There are people who cannot live without their iPod because their minds are already full of negative thoughts, and they always need some kind of distraction to push the negative thoughts away. We do anything to keep our mind away from the stream of negative thinking.

Basic concepts. Irrational thinking can be defined as rigid, inconsistent with reality, illogical, and it interferes with your psychological well-being and gets in the way of pursuing your purpose in life. While rational thinking represents reasonable, objective, flexible and constructive conclusions, or an inference about reality that supports survival, happiness and healthy results. Irrationality can be very harmful, clouding over the conscious with distortions, misconceptions, overgeneralization, and oversimplifications. They limit and narrow our outlook; thus, we repeat mistakes. The core of irrational beliefs is present in destructive conditions such as impulsiveness, arrogance, defeatism, condemnation, depression, anxiety, hostility, insecurity, addiction, procrastination, envy, and compulsive and obsessive thoughts. To sum it up, irrationality/negativity is a serious fatal flaw in our lives.

Suppose a plate of rotten food was spoiling the smell of your room. What would be the best way to get rid of the smell? Should you buy a fan to fan the air in the room, or get rid of the plate of rotten food? The second choice is obviously the one that will be chosen by most rational people. Still, most people do the opposite, just fanning the smell more and more. This is what they do with the management of their problems. They keep visiting them over and over until the neurons of the brain register the negativity, and keep producing it when the situation arises.

Thoughts crowd together just as the birds of the same feather flock together. Negative thoughts join together and attack you. If you entertain good thoughts, all good thoughts join together. Like attracts like. Somehow, humans tend to entertain negative thoughts more than positive ones. Nevertheless, Carl Jung explained in his concept of archetypes that our ancestors suffered in their harsh lives, because of extreme weather, or animal attacks, or the extreme difficult conditions they lived in. All these difficulties have been inherited through our collective unconsciousness, and are manifested in our lives right now.

Psychologists have labeled certain negative thought patterns as cognitive distortions. These are common ways your mind will try to convince you of something that is not actually true. Some of these thoughts are:

A) Obsessive dwelling on an unpleasant event; B) Catastrophizing, seeing the worst in in every situation; C) Taking things personally; D) Blaming others for your problems. Most of us have that kind of thinking, and undoubtedly these thoughts lead to our unhappiness and misery. The sad fact of reality is the majority of us do not try to get rid of such dysfunctional and pathological thoughts.

Do not believe everything you think. Often, our thoughts do not correspond with reality. We have trained the mind to worry over something, even though the possibility of it happening is very slim, but we worry anyway, because we have stored in our unconscious mind a lot of negative materials. Some of them happened to us, some happened to other people, but we tend to store and ruminate over them. Perhaps that comes to us from our ancestors who lived in hardship. Basically, we inherited such memories through the concept of archetypes, which Jung talked about. Our tendencies are toward being negative and toward distortion of reality.

There is a real story that shows why you should not believe everything that comes to your mind. A man was walking down a New York street when he screamed "help, help!" Someone came from behind and stabbed him and killed him. The police talked to witnesses, as a large number of people witnessed the incident. They took the body to autopsy, and it clearly indicated the victim died as a result of stabbing. However, the testimony of witnesses reported completely different statements. Some said he was hit on the head by a rock, others said he was hit by a baseball bat, and still others said he was shot with a rifle. All the testimonies presented completely different pictures from the actual incident.

The interpretation of this is that people do not see reality, they see what is in the mind. For example, if I have a desire to hit someone in the head with a rock, but did not have the opportunity to do so, I bring the desire from the unconscious mind and present, or project it onto a real event. It then becomes real to me without hesitation. This is why we say do not believe yourself, because your unconscious mind may present not actual experiences, but what the has been stored for many years. Tania Kotsos said "Mind your reality, as it is in the eyes of the beholder. Change the invisible, and the visible will follow."

Besides years of psychoanalysis, is there anything we can do to change negative thought patterns? As the '90s book said, you cannot afford the luxury of negative thoughts. Your thoughts are powerful, and create chemicals in your brain either adding or subtracting from your brain's power, health, ability to cope with life, and happiness. Meditation can be a great tool to quiet the mind, and thousands and thousands of studies indicate meditation can be a very effective tool to quiet the mind and regulate our disturbing thoughts.

Thought power is the key to creating your reality; everything you perceive in the physical world has its origin in the invisible, which is the inner world of your thoughts and beliefs. You need to learn to control the nature of your dominant, habitual thoughts. Put another way, the conditions and circumstances of your life are a result of your collective thoughts and beliefs. As James Allen said, "circumstances do not make a man, they reveal him."

Positive thoughts. The Encarta Dictionary (2003), defines positive as confident, optimistic and focusing on good things rather than bad. Therefore, positive thoughts are sets of ideas in the mind that bring confidence, optimism, and focus to an individual.

But, the nature of the mind is to be suspicious and critical. If someone does 99 good things and 1 bad thing, the mind will invariably remember the bad thing. If we allow ourselves to be drawn into highlighting our mistakes, we will invite more negative mindset. Let's take a common irrational belief many of us share, that if things are not the way we expect them to be, they are terrible. Such a belief actually leads to disappointment and refusal to accept difficult or challenging circumstances. It is also our negative self-talk, influenced by an irrational fear of not being good enough. It is an overgeneralization that we tend to have about ourselves because we did not succeed in some endeavors.

What the experts and pundits say. Thomas Bucker said, "Being in a good frame of mind helps keep one in the picture of health," while Bill Clinton said, "Running helps me stay on an even keel and in an optimistic frame of mind." As Aristotle said, "Happiness is not a condition that is produced or stands on its own; rather, it is a frame of mind that accompanies an activity."

George F. Will: "Frame of mind is a steely determination to do well." Every dark cloud has a silver lining. Nelson Mandela: "I learned that courage was not the absence of fear, but the triumph over it. The brave man is not he who does not feel afraid, but he who conquers the fear."

Thoughts are developed according to our expectations and core beliefs. Some of our core beliefs may influence us positively, like building self-esteem or trust toward others. Other core beliefs may influence us negatively, fostering negative self-esteem, irrational fears and unrealistic expectations. It is so easy to get into a negative mindset which invariably leads to unhappiness and depression. To avoid being overwhelmed by negativity we need to make a conscious effort to avoid the experiences that reinforce a negative frame of mind.

We are surrounded by negativity. Pick up newspapers or turn on the television and you will be bombarded with shocking images and bad news. Why do we take notice and keep feeding these negative thoughts? That is the way our minds have been trained and programmed for thousands of years. The inherited wisdom of the mind is only restrained by the remnants of an animal heritage of destructive emotion. Basically we are unhappy folks, and it comes from a pre-instilled mindset.

There is a mammalian root to our emotions. It has been built on fear in the jungle. Dan King and Chris Janiszewski wrote, "human affective systems evolved from mammalian affective systems." To have a positive frame of mind in today's world can be a challenge of monumental proportions. If you are in a negative state of mind, you will create a pot of deception, which may lead almost to paranoia. Sadly that is the current human condition.

Irrational thoughts are something that plague us all from time to time and can cause a lot of problems. These are the kind of thoughts that make us worried that something bad may happen to ourselves or to loved ones. Such irrational thoughts come from negative emotion, rather than from logic. And often, they are not congruent with the real world. They are faulty thoughts, and as such they stop us from going about our daily lives, or make our lives a painful journey.

The core of the trouble with such thoughts is they are self-perpetuating and confirming. Negative thoughts mean simply you are human. Life throws us twists and turns that can be unsettling, disturbing, and frightening. Most of us have to go through struggle, frustrations, and even a nightmarish situation at some point in life. It is normal to feel bad or negative; if you deny such thoughts that is not natural. However, do not let such feelings hold you back from moving forward. We must not let our addiction to irrational thinking make our lives as a living hell.

If you have an irrational thought, that will definitely affect your behavior, and you will act to reinforce your belief. For instance, if you worry that everyone will look at you, you act oddly or nervous, and then everyone <u>does</u> look at you. If you feel it's too dangerous to be outside, you stay inside and] confirm that irrational thought, rather than challenging it. The next time you have that thought, it will be stronger because it is now backed up by your experiences. These thoughts can build up to serious disorders like phobias, depression, anxiety, paranoia and even schizophrenia.

In anxiety disorders, the disturbance is coming from the mind, which is playing tricks on you and betraying you. Dan Shapiro, in his book, *Life is a Fork in the Road*, indicated that negative thoughts drain you of energy and keep you from being in the present. The more you give in to your negative thoughts, the stronger they become. Stop feeding the monster inside of your head, as it will become so fat, and eventually will swallow you. I think the majority of us have been swallowed by the monster of negativity occasionally, or for entire lifetimes, meaning we are chronically negative. I am sure you have encountered people in life who they are so negative and complain about anything and everything.

As is said, "we are what we think." Thinking is a natural process, from the time we awake until we go to sleep. But incessant thoughts robotically arise and subside in our mind without respite. The majority of these thoughts are useless and negative. These thoughts deplete our energy and lead to stress, restlessness, anxiety, and mental fatigue, as well as eventually to poor health, and take all the joy from our lives.

Scientists say there is a neurological reason for the cycle of negative thinking we all sometimes fall into. When the amygdale -- the part of the brain which plays a key role in emotion -- becomes aroused, it remains in that state for a long time. At the same time, memories of the situation that aroused it become imprinted in the brain. The more emotion we exhibit, the stronger the memory will be, and over time, a specific memory becomes attached to a certain emotion.

How do negative thoughts develop? Our upbringing may be at the source of the tendency to have negative thoughts more frequently than others. Parenting style can be imprinted on our mind, because we copy our parents' behavior. Criticism from parents can also lead to the adoption of a negative mental framework. Sometimes the circumstances in which we find ourselves, with no exit, leads to this, like the situations in Iraq or Syria. Inevitability people become negative and hostile toward the world around them, as well as toward themselves.

Barbara Fredrickson, in her book *Positivism*, suggests that positive emotions evolved to promote activities like exploration, learning, relationship building, and investment in future activities that are often eschewed in times of stress for an organism, while negative emotions narrow our focus and enable us to deal effectively with immediate threats or challenges. A positive frame of mind is important to boost performance and quality of life. There are some biological explanations for this. A positive frame of mind is triggered by enhanced levels of neurotransmitters such as serotonin that regulate the performance capabilities of the brain, which leads to better physical and mental health.

Common signs of negative thinking. The worst sign of negative thinking is the internal chatter replaying negative events in your head, or gossip, or fear of the worst, or expecting bad over good when we are faced with situations. If you beat yourself up for being too negative, you are simply reinforcing the pattern, not breaking out of it. People in general are stuck in negative thinking, and remain stuck until they experience an evolution in their consciousness, because life always reflects back the content of our consciousness.

We also worry over what people may think of us. Mahatma Gandhi challenged that thought by saying, "I will not let anyone walk through my mind with their dirty feet." You have no control over what people may feel or think of you, thus, "you cannot direct the wind but you can adjust the sails."

You have to adjust your perception and interpretations of people's behavior to suit you and calm your mind. Some people may see their lives as a perpetual dark tunnel, and all they need is to learn to change their outlook.

Negative thoughts and emotion give life to each other. Charles F. Haanel, in his book *Mental Chemistry*, explained the inexorable effect our thoughts have on emotions by comparing emotions to the fluidity of water. Suppose you have a tube of water and stir that water in a circular motion. If you stir long enough and with enough force, the water will have enough force behind it to temporarily move whatever you are stirring it with. And, it will be noticeably difficult to stir that water in the opposite direction, because of the initial resistance caused by the ongoing momentum.

Our emotions are like flowing water and your thoughts stir them toward either positivism or negativity. The intensity and the rate at which you repeat a thought determines the intensity and the strength of the emotion that correlates to it. And the more forceful your emotions flow in a particular direction, the stronger the initial resistance when you try to change the direction of that movement by thinking opposing thoughts.

You have probably heard that positive thinking will change negative emotion to positive emotion. But you have tried this approach and it did not always work for you as well as you hoped. The momentum of those negative emotions is to strong, because of the constant punctuation of negative subconscious thoughts that are continually giving power to them. Undoubtedly, positive thinking will change the physical composition of your mind over time, and should obviously be taken seriously. But it will not stop the cycle of negative thoughts and emotions as immediately as another approach will.

Lao Tzu suggested, "Stop thinking, and end your problems." The most practical action you could possibly take to resolve this issue is to simply stop thinking. When you are already in a negative frame of mind, you are going to have a natural inclination to think along the same lines hose emotions are guiding you. You may think that trying to rationalize your problems while in this frame of mind will increase your understanding of them. But this approach will only lead to you feeling worse about yourself, because you are focusing on your problems while negative emotions have their influence over you. So break this cycle by stopping your thoughts entirely until this negative feeling goes away. With nothing to feed them, they will gradually lose their strength, like water that has ceased to be actuated. If you do this, you will experience a new level of mental freedom.

From time to time we let negative experiences affect our lives. They catch us off guard, the mental pictures from these experiences repeat themselves in our mind, and we feel disheartened or worried about them all day, all week or even all our life. Negative emotion can cause detrimental changes to the biochemistry of our bodies by releasing stress hormones. These stress hormones can slow down our rate of digestion, cause our blood pressure to rise, weaken our heart, cause life-threatening disease and accelerate the signs of aging. Scientific research indicates that ongoing negative trauma can even alter the genes in our DNA, causing adverse effects in our offspring for two generations.

True positive thinking is not the absence of negative thoughts. Positive thinking is the type of focus that can help you achieve your goals, overcome adversity, and realize your full potential. But it does not mean the avoidance of negative thoughts. Positive thinking is the ability to feel negative when you have to, and still maintain enough hope to keep on going.

Some schools of thought say we should try to turn negative thoughts into positive ones. That is impossible, because that denies our very nature. We as humans are frail, imperfect, mistake-prone beings who can react in an emotional way to what happens to us. Positive thinking starts by embracing reality; true positive thoughts do not deny the reality or try to sugarcoat the difficulty. Try not calling it a problem, and call it an opportunity, just to give it a good spin. Do not exaggerate it, just address what you face and define it accurately.

The great thinkers of existential thoughts (Soren Kierkegaard, Blaise Pascal, Albert Camus, Martin Heidegger, Karl Jaspers, and Nietzsche) suggested that the chief problem, as observed by those with their eyes and minds wide open, was it's necessary for modern man to believe in something. That something was an ordering principle and was necessary, because the scientific temperament seemed not to satisfy man, but to cause him to wander even more aimlessly. Mankind needed a new book of lessons, and a teacher as well. Humanity demanded it, and what happened to produce such a yearning was, man had recognized his nihilistic tendencies. Man is alone because he cannot communicate with others. He finds himself in a world in which he is utterly alien to others and to himself. The world has no purpose and no meaning, according to existential views.

They see modern man is mechanical, robotic, conformist, confused and alienated. Man is little more than a cog in a grand machine which man himself has produced, and we kneel before the great machine, yearning for liberation, only to be rewarded with imprisonment in our own mind. Given this rather unpleasant scenario, anxiety, depression, and fears may lead to nihilism and death. So, what is the point to being here? Man has been shackled by authority with political or religious intentions. Man is an ambiguous creature.

The existential views go further to see existence as not rational, but absurd. We have invented reason to shield ourselves against fears, and to rationalize the most irrational thinking. As William Butler Yeats once wrote, "we cannot know the truth, but we can live it." That is our place in the world. As the existential thinker put it, our existence is little more than a cruel trick. Even King Solomon suggested that life is irrational, absurd and meaningless. Undoubtedly, the existential view of mankind and our purpose to be on the earth is ludicrous and cynical. Let's go with their logic though. Since they see life as absurd, then why do we take life so seriously and torture ourselves over what has gone wrong? We need to enjoy the ride even if it's a bumpy road. Since we are on the earth, then we need to enjoy it and never take it seriously by any means.

Fundamental suggestions to change our outlook in life:

1) We should feel that a negative mindset is a choice. If we feel a victim to our own emotions and thoughts, nobody else will be able to help us. We may feel that because we are holding onto a negative frame of mind, we inevitably are choosing to be unhappy. Negativity is a conscious decision which leads to misery. If we really value the importance of our own inner peace and happiness, we will aspire to cultivate this through good, uplifting thoughts.

2) Spend time doing activities. The best antidote to negativity is simply to spend time doing positive, uplifting activities. Sometimes if we analyze and examine our own negativity we do nothing to reduce it. By engaging in useful fun activities, we forget about the reasons for our negativity. Do not sit around doing nothing; the worst thing for a negative frame of mind is to mope around feeling sorry for ourselves, or ruminating on our bad luck, and worrying. In such a case fears will

not diminish. But if we spend time in exercise and activities, that can be a powerful way to bring about a new level of healthy consciousness.

3) Spend time with positive people. The world has no shortage of negative people; try to be around uplifting, encouraging, positive and compassionate people. That will shape your perception and reinforce positive thinking in you. Do not be around complainers, they drown your energy and leave you with emptiness. Moreover, complaining is like taking a bath in dirty water. It gets into the fabric of your neurons and bathes you with negativity. Thus, when you are around people who complain, try to run away from them to save your neurons from a dirty bath.

4) Do not accept negativity from other people. We live in a world where there is no shortage of pessimists, critics, and people who are "downers". There will always be people who can find the negative in life, but there is no reason why we have to ascribe to their world views.

5) Let go of thoughts. If you can learn to control your thoughts, you can control experiences and emotion of life. Maybe the antidote to negativity is to learn prayer and meditation. Force yourself to think of three positive thoughts. When your mind starts wandering and swimming in negativity, try to remember a few good things that you have done in your life. Norman Vincent Peale put it elegantly: "There is a basic law that like attracts like." Negative thinking definitely attracts negative results. Conversely, if a person habitually thinks optimistically and hopefully, his positive thinking sets in motion creative forces and success, and make his life a pleasurable journey.

6) Do not think anything you would not say in front of people. We often think things we would never say in front of people. If you are annoyed or disappointed with yourself, try to put on a positive face and pretend you are fine.

7) Have a plan for your life. Life is not easy; a range of interpersonal, career and health problems is a fact of life. When setbacks occur, stomach churning emotions give you sleepless nights and affect your health. Such emotions are only suitable for a life in the jungle. Unfortunately our mind has not adjusted to the more civilized world.

8) Read inspiring books. There are thousands of books packed with the experiences and wisdom of people and they can be very uplifting to your spirit.

9) Keep a gratitude journal. You have to make a conscious decision to dwell on the positive things in your life, and try to avoid slipping into a negative frame of mind.

10) Eat healthy food. Avoid processed food, exercise regularly, challenge your lazy tendencies, and take a walk in nature.

11) Limit TV watching, and make those limits an integral part of your life. Normally, the media tends to present the negative view of our reality, and often, ignores the creative part. Since we cannot do anything about the bad news, it is best not to see it. So do not allow a dosage of negativity to get into our system, and ruin our health.

Means to overcome irrational thoughts.

1) 1) Mindfulness -- it is one of the strategies that is used in CBT. You watch the stream of thoughts running into your mind, but you do not hold them; you watch them like a cloud going by in the sky. This will allow you to identify the faulty thoughts that are causing damage, and by recognizing them, you can then try to make sure you do not think them again in the future.

2) Affirmations -- you can use a positive statement to replace a negative statement. You need to be diligent and post the statement all over your living space so you can drill it into your mind.

3) Write things down. You need to focus on writing the things down; for example, you may receive 10 compliments and 1 insult. So you tend to focus on the insult and ignore the compliments, and that will damage your self-esteem. Try to read back to yourself what you write. This way you will reinforce the positive things instead of focusing on the negative ones, and it will become concrete evidence for your experiences.

4) Challenge your thoughts -- when the negative/irrational thoughts come to your mind, try to prove them wrong. Of course, that requires some courage, but once you do it, you will feel good about yourself.

5) Do the thing that you fear and the death of fear is certain. This is the wisdom of the ages; if you avoid the thing that you fear, that will reinforce your view of yourself as a failure. Challenge yourself and go for it. Then you will taste the joy of overcoming the thing you fear. For

example, if you have a fear of speaking in public, take any opportunity to speak in front of people, and gradually you will become a master of public speaking.

6) Smile, it is a real help to change your mood.

7) Do not play the victim. You are the creator of your life, so take responsibility.

8) Help someone else, and try to shift the focus from your internal conflicts to the external help of other people. It can be a miracle for you. As Jesus said, "in order to find yourself, get out of yourself."

Eliminating the irrational/negative frame of thinking:

1) Identify your irrational thinking and put it down on paper.

2) Have a daily movement meditation, which means that you focus on what you're doing right at that specific moment.

3) Keep yourself busy in meaningful activities, such as exercise, writing, playing music and in other meaningful activities.

4) When negative thoughts enter your mind, try not to fight them; just bring some positive thoughts to replace them. If you fight them, you may give them more power.

5) Be around positive, encouraging people.

6) Do not allow people to treat you badly; be assertive in what you want, and remember to treat others the way you want to be treated.

7) When you are faced with difficulty in your life; try to ask for help from people who know how to help you out.

8) Cherish yourself as a human being and never put a price tag on yourself. Do not attach your self-esteem to your performance. We all are capable of doing something and incapable of doing something else.

9) Look beyond yourself, and see the world as place to enjoy. Be happy when you are by yourself, as well as with others.

10) Be clear that you are on a short journey on this earth and your purpose is to be happy. If you veer from that direction, then you have to try to seek some professional help, to restore your sense of purpose and balance in your life.

Chapter Seventeen

Intrusive Thoughts: OCD

Intrusive thoughts are defined as unwelcome, involuntary thoughts, images, or unpleasant ideas that may become obsessive. They usually involve inappropriate things at inappropriate times, and are associated with anxiety disorders. Those thoughts may be paralyzing. People with anxiety or depression often suffer with repetitive scary, uncomfortable racing thoughts. With obsessive thinking, an exhausted mind will hold onto thoughts that seem scary, unnatural or even obscene. If we use a metaphor to define OCD, it is like a tidal wave that crashes through our minds and washes away all other concerns. We may become obsessed with a person, place, a goal, or a subject, but obsession amounts to the same thing in all cases.

Obsession can be a form of addiction to thoughts. Obsession is intoxication; it fills up the mind and it makes you devalue important dimensions of life, and tolerate their atrophy and even their collapse. It is like brick walls that form a prison around your mind; the harder you try to get rid of them, the more powerful they become.

The intrusive thought comes from outside of our control, and their content feels alien and threatening. For some people, intrusive thoughts are part and parcel of panic, or intrusive anxiety. They result from anxiety, and they add more fear to the anxiety you are already experiencing.

Mental factors associated with intrusive thoughts include: feeling, recognition, mental impulses, concentration, attention, contact, connection of an object with the mind, ignorance, attachment, desire, anger, pride, inflated superiority, doubt, wrong views, speculative delusions and being in two minds about reality.

When we experience intrusive thoughts, it is like being forced to watch a horror movie, and as if we can never escape. The intrusive memory is stored sensory data, and in your mind it is merely a stored impulse from the body.

The universe can only be observed through a brain, and it is largely interpreted subjectively.

Why do thoughts pop into our head? Barry Gordon said we are aware of a tiny fraction of the thinking that goes on in the mind. The intrusive thoughts you experience illustrate the disconcerting fact that many of the functions of the mind are outside of conscious control. Whether we maintain true control over any mental functions is the central debate about free will. Perhaps this lack of autonomy is to be expected, as the foundation for almost all the mind's labors were laid long before our ancestors developed an evolved consciousness.

Even deliberate decisions are not completely under our power. Our awareness only sets the start and the end of a goal, but leaves the implementation to unconscious mental processes. Often all kind of thoughts are simmering in our preconscious until they gather sufficient strength to pop into awareness.

Toxic thoughts. Dr. Caroline Leaf indicated 75% to 95% of illnesses that plague us today are a direct result of our thoughts. It is oxic emotion that affects us and brings us to illness. The average person has more than 30,000 thoughts a day, and most are uncontrollable. For example, fear triggers more than 1,400 known physical and chemical responses, and activates more than 30 different hormones. Toxic waste generated by toxic thoughts causes diabetes, cancer, asthma, skin problems and allergies, to name just a few. Medical research shows that thinking and consciously controlling our mind is the best way to detoxify our brain. However, the mind tends to then produce a new idea; it is a definite process.

In obsessive thinking, you are fighting your mind with the mind, the thought is an energy form created in the mind. You cannot use the mind to stop the mind a sword cannot cut itself). If you ask yourself how to stop a negative thought, this is another thought. Everyone feel anxious, fearful, uncertain, or worried at some time in their lives. In OCD the mind's filter for sorting out what is dangerous from what is not is not working properly. Instead of keeping normal worry in perspective, OCD tends to exaggerate fears, and keeps your mind in a constant stream of uncertainty, doubt, and fear.

People with OCD feel strong urges to do certain things repeatedly, called rituals or compulsions. They want to banish the scary thought or ward it off, but the thought keeps coming. People with OCD feel a brief sense of relief when they do a compulsion, but the compulsion actually strengthens the OCD thoughts and encourages them to return. The more someone performs the compulsion, the stronger the illness becomes. The obsessive mind can generate a cycle of suffering thoughts. OCD relates to the level of serotonin. When the flow is blocked, the brain's "alarm system" overreacts.

We are lost in the terrains of our mind. Often, we give power to thoughts by having interest in them, and that interest, in turn, is the fuel of the thoughts. Do not get involved in your thoughts and try to disassociate yourself from them. Often the mind likes to ruminate on negative events, not positive ones. Why are we infected with tragic thoughts? The answer lies with our ancestors who used to be afraid of animals, suffer from heat, cold and various illnesses. Their lives were very hard and often constant struggles; thus, we have inherited the tendency of being negative from them. The mind has a pernicious habit of externalizing things to avoid responsibility. It also exaggerates fears and dramatizes events, as if building a castle in the air. Hideous thoughts come to our mind in spite of our refusal.

People are struggling in their heads, without any change in their visible behavior. We still do not know why some people get OCD, and some do not. One fact we do know: if you struggle with the thoughts in your head, you definitely make it stronger.

Our negative thinking is insidious. If your desires, expectations, wishes, and ambitions are not fulfilled, you will be depressed, anxious and stressed. "I think I think …I think. I have thought myself out of happiness a million times, but never once into it." (Jonathan Foer). The mind is only a bundle of thoughts and like water; it follows a familiar direction. Since you worry, the mind moves in that direction. Much as your body is built from the food you eat, your mind is built from the experiences you have.

Deepak Chopra, in his article *A Freer, Happier Way to Think*, stated that every day, unwanted thoughts enter our minds. Undoubtedly, our minds are vulnerable to negative thoughts, causing us doubt, worry, and anxiety. Frequently, it is the same negative thoughts that return over and over. Repetition is a sign indicating something is wrong in the process of your thinking and you need to change. There is a part of you calling out to get your attention.

These thoughts are like having a rock in your shoe. It is not reasonable to ask the rock to quit hurting you, or to see it as your enemy. The pain the rock causes is only asking for remedy. You are stuck in your mental misery, not because of thoughts, but because of the lack of a viable strategy. Psychologists have asserted that there is a huge difference between having negative thoughts, and turning them into action. Thought is fleeting mental images, they have no consequences until you choose to make them important. Try to take the mental rock out of your mind by:

1) Turn negative into positive action. When you see a crying child, you rush to help. Similarly, you are crying for help. When you have obsessive thoughts, center yourself, sit quietly, and ask yourself, what is scaring me? Use the rational part of your brain, and do not give way to runaway emotion, and design a solution.

2) Get a healthy outside perspective, because when you are in a forest, it is difficult for you to see the trees. In this case, you may seek a competent psychologist, with a firm sense of self, lack of fears, and plenty of self-reliance, who can provide you with a different fresh perspective about life in general. Obsessions can result from a conflict over sexuality, or as a means of aggression, or it can be guilt feelings directed at oneself.

Jeffrey Schwartz, who has investigated obsessive intrusive thoughts, indicated this thought process is the most debilitating mental illness in our time. For example, look what obsessive thoughts did to Howard Hughes, who went from being a genius billionaire to a shaggy recluse; a miserable person who was caught in the grip of obsessive-compulsive disorder. Schwartz indicated that in his book *Brain Lock: Free Yourself from Obsessive-Compulsive Behavior*. Obsessive thinking manifests in a wide variety of problematic behaviors, such as compulsive hand washing, door opening, repetitive checking of the ovens and the door, repetition of the same thoughts over and over, or even the fear of death and illness.

The origin of OCD is at the neurological level, where hyper-connectivity between two brain regions, the orbitofrontal cortex and the caudate nucleus (the habit center of the brain), create a tidal wave of unfounded mortal fear, triggering habitual response as the only way to attain calm. The worst part is that despite recognition that these thoughts and behavior are irrational, the OCD sufferer feels driven to obey them.

OCD contradicts the notion of free will, which suggests an ever-increasing number of our choices are somehow hardwired into us, from the spouse we choose to the flavor of ice cream we like. David Eagleman and Sam

Harris wrote a wonderful book to explain that we are, at the root of it, high functioning delusional robots.

There are four steps in the treatment of OCD. The basic principle is to understand these thoughts and urges. Managing fear, in turn, allows you to control your behavioral response much more effectively. In these techniques, we use the biological method and cognitive awareness much more effectively. There are four treatment strategies: re-label, reattribute, refocus, and revalue.

Re-label. The critical step is to recognize obsessive thoughts and compulsive urges. You must gain an understanding that the feeling is bothersome. Make mental notes, like "this thought is obsessive; I must be conscious and mindful of the urge." For example, "I do not think that my hand is dirty, yet I am having a compulsive urge to wash my hand." You have to be an impartial spectator.

The goal of this step is to relabel intrusive thoughts and urges in your own mind as obsessive and compulsive, and to do it assertively. Tell yourself it is a false alarm, with no base in reality. The goal of this stage is to control the response, not the thought or the urge behind it.

Reattribution. It is not me, it is my OCD. It is not meaningful, my hands are not dirty, but the thought is strong, and does not go away. The discomforts are due to a biochemical imbalance in the *caudate nucleus* and the *putamen* next to it. During a normal day, we make many rapid shifts of behavior without thinking about them; in OCD, efficient filtering and shifting thoughts and behavior are disrupted by a glitch in the caudate nucleus.

As a result of this malfunction, the front of the brain becomes overactive and uses excessive energy. It is like having your car stuck in a ditch, in gear. The core of this stage is to not act. Do not take your thoughts at face value. Do not listen to them; they are false messages from the brain. Put the thoughts aside and move to another behavior. Avoid being a sucker and establishing the false habit of OCD each time. Usually the first stage and this stage can be performed together.

Refocus. The idea here is to shift your attention, and focus on something else. If only for few minutes, choose a specific behavior or thought; take a walk or play music, read a book, or exercise. Say to yourself, "I am experiencing symptoms of OCD, I need to have another behavior." Try to reclaim your decision and tell yourself the OCD is no longer running the show.

Immediately try to take 15 minutes off, never performing OCD behaviors. Then after this do a pleasant, constructive behavior longer than 15 minutes, even half an hour, the longer the better. Having mindful activities will empower you; do not let yourself crumble under bizarre and seemingly inexplicable forces. Never respond to the urge of OCD, or allow it to determine what you do. Have a mental picture about what you do, so the OCD cannot force itself on you. Try to keep a record of your success at refocusing time.

Revalue. In this stage you use the concept of the impartial spectator, the person inside of us who is aware of our feelings. Try to change your behavior, then you feel the change. Who is in charge of your behavior, you or the OCD? It is not worth it to go with a silly urge. Try not to ruminate or fantasize about the consequences of acting out obsessive thoughts. Take charge of your life; be mindful when you give in to an urge, you lose personal mastery and the art of self-command. Once you trivialize the intrusive thought, you enhance self-esteem and take back your life. That will lead to a change in your brain chemistry. The consequence of such change is life-affirming action and true freedom.

What is a pure obsession? It is a compulsion that takes place internally. OCD victims often suffer in silence. People think they are flawed internally as a result of evil or psychotic thoughts. The human brain naturally generates nonsensical and often bizarre thoughts. Often, people have violent or forbidden thoughts. There are many ways an individual can engage in mental compulsions, such as anti-religious thoughts, persistent doubt, or somatic functions. You could become wrapped up in this process for most of a day.

Thought and reality are not the same. If they were, you would be rich. Think about a pot of gold all day long, and pray for it. At the end of the day, all you have are a lot of thoughts, and you cannot take your thoughts to the bank.

Leo Tolstoy described a game he played when he was a child in Russia. He would stand in the corner and not think about a white bear. Years later Harvard psychologist Dan Wegner showed that people instructed not to think about a white bear were more likely to think about white bears. Thought suppression leads to thought rebound.

Overcoming obsessive thoughts requires patience and persistence so you can bring balance to life. There are steps you can take to break the repetitive cycle. However, it is easier to adjust to compulsions, which you can see, rather than obsessions, which you cannot. But often, obsession fuels compulsion.

1) <u>Revisualization</u>. Whenever obsessive thoughts run through your mind, use humor or stupidity to downplay those thoughts and make them less frightening.

2) <u>Positive self-talk</u>. Do not over value the thoughts, and have reassurance that you do not carry or accept those thoughts, and that neutralizes them.

3) <u>Shrink the chatter box</u>. See your obsessive thoughts as nothing but a loud chatter box that never shuts up, and the more it irritates you, the stronger and louder it gets. You can shrink the chatter box simply by accepting and downsizing the importance of what it is saying, and it will fade into the background and become less important to you.

4) <u>Thought-stopping techniques</u> are highly effective. Most people experience random thoughts on a regular basis; they do not mean anything. They just come and go. However, the sensitive person tends to be anxious about such thoughts, and once they analyze such thoughts, they will become stronger. If you do not pay attention to them, they tend to fade away.

5) <u>Focus on what makes you anxious</u>, and try not to engage in your thoughts.

6) <u>Do not trust your feelings</u> when you deal with obsessive thoughts. Obsession is a great bluffer; it may tell you that you are in danger, when you are perfectly safe.

7) <u>Do not talk back</u>, do not use logic. The thoughts just become stronger; do not give them power.

8) <u>Know it will pass</u>, and do not act on it., Have a "cooling off" period.

9) <u>Focus on now</u>. Keep yourself busy doing things at hand, not giving in to obsessive thoughts.

10) <u>Do something else</u>, and distract yourself from obsessive thoughts.

11) <u>Blame the chemistry</u> inside your head; say your head is wired to ruminate. There is no catastrophic problem that needs to be solved in the next 24 hours.

12) <u>Picture it</u>. Visualize and ridicule the thought.

If you follow these steps as written, and the other materials in this chapter regarding obsessive thinking, I assure you, you will overcome it and it will become part of the past. Apply yourself sincerely and try not to excuse yourself, because the whole goal of life is to be happy and free from disturbing thoughts.

Chapter Eighteen

Pathological Thinking

Before we indulge in knowing the pathology of our thinking, there are questions to be answered: How does our brain work?

How do we resolve the mysteries of our mind? What we comprehend, is based on the limitation of our brain. The general principle of understanding the human brain is how information is stored, recalled, and processed. No two brains are alike, and even your brain a few years ago is different than it is now. The ability to question lies at the root of thinking; when we truly think, and do not just mimic what another person tells us, the activity arises out of questioning. It is the driving force of any thought process. You must learn to question yourself and the world around you, because most of us have no idea how we know what we know.

The mind carries on the battle of the cognitive revolution. The finest achievements of the species have been attributed to it. It is said to work at miraculous speeds in miraculous ways. Perception, ideas, feelings, intentions, all of these are the property of the mind. The other battle of the mind is, why does the mind keep close bad experiences and tends to forget good experiences? Is that part of human inclination?

Today, the answer is becoming clear to us: it is because of the pathology of our ancestors, who suffered]the hardships of life. Another explanation as to why people have a tendency toward negativity, not positivity, is that this is part of our psychic makeup. In other words, we are suckers.

We like to inflict pain on others and ourselves. For example, there is normal marital sadism, a mutual ongoing emotional torture. It is a very common, though rarely acknowledged experience in a relationship. Normal marital sadism runs the gamut, from overt loud fighting, to passive forms of aggression (Otto Fenichel). It is a form of thought pathology, but people never admit it, because it may uncover our ugly nature as far as commitment and relationships are concerned.

There are a few concepts which we may relate to the pathology of our thoughts, and we need to understand them, as they are considered to be components of thought. For example, what do we mean by perception? It is the ability to see, hear, or become aware of something through the senses. It is the archaeology of thoughts. Thinking is often a weaker word for knowing.

Our brain can fathom the beginning of time and the end of the universe, but is the brain capable of understanding itself? With billions of neurons, each with thousands of connections, one's noggin is a complex and congested mental freeway. Neurologists and cognitive scientists today are probing how the mind gives rise to thoughts, actions, emotions, and ultimately consciousness.

Norman Weinberger, neuroscientist at the University of California - Irvine said, "If we understand the brain, we will understand both its capacities and its limits for thought, emotion, reasoning, love and every other aspect of human life." Scott Hurtle at Duke University sees the brain as the most complex object in the known universe. Complexity makes simple models impractical and accurate models impossible to comprehend. He also indicated the real snag in brain science is one of "navel gazing", whereby we cannot step outside of our own brain and experiences, when studying the brain itself.

We all think we understand the brain, at least our own thoughts and experiences. But our own subjective experiences are a very poor guide to knowing how the brain works. According to Hurtle, whether the human brain can understand itself is one of the oldest philosophical questions.

The Pathology of Thinking. Pathology is used to designate thinking that is imbalanced by emotion; it tends to vary in nature:

1) Egocentric memory. There is a natural tendency within us to forget evidence and information that does not support our current thinking, and remember evidence and information that does.

2) Egocentric myopia. There is a natural tendency to think in an absolutist way within a point of view.

3) Egocentric righteousness. There is a natural tendency to feel superior in light of our confidence that we possess the truth, when we do

not. That is the type of thinking that most terrorists operate from, believing they are right, and everybody else is wrong.

4) Egocentric hypocrisy. There is a natural tendency to ignore flagrant inconsistent behavior or attitudes. For example, between what we profess to believe and the actual belief our behavior implies, or between the standard to which we hold ourselves and that to which we hold others.

5) Egocentric oversimplification, a natural tendency to ignore real and important complexities in the world in favor of simplistic notions, when consideration of those complexities would require us to modify our beliefs or values.

6) Egocentric blindness, the natural tendency not to notice facts and evidence that contradicts our favored beliefs or values. These type of thoughts are common in the Arab world.

7) Egocentric immediacy, which is the tendency to overgeneralize immediate feelings and experiences. When one event in our life is highly favorable or unfavorable, all our life seems favorable or unfavorable to us.

8) Egocentric absurdity, the natural tendency to fail to notice thinking that has absurd consequences.

Hallucinations. Hallucinations are false or distorted sensory expressions that appear to be vertical (true) perception. These sensory impressions are generated by the mind rather than by any external stimuli, and may be seen, heard, felt and even smelled or tasted.

Hallucinations occur when environmental, emotional, or physical factors, such as stress, medication, extreme fatigue, or mental illness, cause the mechanism within the brain that distinguishes conscious perceptions from internal memory-based perception to misfire. As a result, hallucination occurs during periods of consciousness. They can appear in the form of visions, or sounds, tactile feelings (known as haptic hallucination), smells, or tastes.

Delusion. Delusion is a false belief based on incorrect inference about external reality that is firmly sustained, despite what almost everybody else believes and despite incontrovertible and obvious proof to the contrary. The belief is not one ordinarily accepted by other members of the person's culture or subculture.

Illusion is a misperception or misinterpretation of a real external stimulus, such as hearing the rustling of leaves as the sound of a voice.

Archaic thinking is an old pattern of thinking the focuses on the past, as well as having a certain amount of nostalgia. Since the individual is unable to cope with the present state of thinking, he or she may resort to archaic thinking, to give him or her some psychological comfort. The Arab people are fixated on the past; thus, they always dwell on how the past was beautiful, and people were happy, which is not true.

Magical thinking is an irrational belief passed on to us or others. Missing the obvious often hurts more than seeing the imaginary, but our skills at inferring connections are overturned. We have magical thinking because we hate surprise, and we love being in control.

Emotional stress and events of personal significance push us strongly toward magical thinking. Dr. Eugene Subbotsky, a Lancaster University psychologist, tells a story about an event in Moscow. He was walking with his son down a long empty block. Suddenly a parked car started moving on its own, then swerved toward them, and finally struck an iron gate just centimeters away. They escaped death very narrowly. He kept thinking magically about this episode. Although I am a rational and scientific man, there are certain phenomena which cannot be explained rationally.

There are many layers of beliefs for magical thinking. There is superstitious ideation, and it turns out no matter how rational people consider themselves to be, they place a high value on hunches and intuition. Or, they will consider an object as sacred, like a wedding ring. They may give invisible meaning to these objects.

The other sacred object that we place incredible values on, and is a part of magical thinking, is the national flag. It is a piece of fabric to which we assign values. We salute the flag and bow to the flag as if it is real and has a spirit, or we derive energy from raising the flag. Unfortunately, humans are really foolish and ridiculous, because millions of people rallied around a flag and lost their lives. We have all seen demonstrations where people put the flag on the ground and step on it, as an insult.

Part of magical thinking is mind over matter. For example, wishing for something is probably the most ubiquitous kind of magical spell around. It's an unreasonable expectation that your thoughts have a force and energy to act on the world, and yet we do not resist such thoughts for fear of jinxing ourselves.

Most cultures around the world also believe that certain rituals bring good luck. Often, we witness the mindless repetition of action with no proven causal effect. We see that on the athletic field. People who truly trust in their rituals exhibit a phenomenon known as illusion of control, the belief that they have more influence over the world than they actually do. It is not necessarily a bad illusion to have, as it offers a sense of control, encouraging people to work harder than they might otherwise.

Psychologist Marjaana Lindeman at the University of Helsinki defined magical thinking as treating the world as if it has mental properties (animism), or expecting the mind to exhibit the properties of the physical world. An example is the belief in Feng Shui, the idea that the arrangement of furniture can channel life energy in the house. It is still a common practice in Chinese culture.

How do we differentiate between magical thinking, positive psychology and psychosis? Magical thinking can be plotted on a spectrum with skeptics at one end and schizophrenics at the other. People who endorse magical ideas, ranging from the innocuous to the outlandish, are more likely to have psychosis, or develop it later in life. People who suffer from OCD also exhibit elevated levels of paranoia, perceptual disturbance, and magical thinking, particularly the thought-action fusion. These people are compelled to carry out repetitive tasks to counteract their intrusive thoughts about unlocked doors or loved ones getting sick. But magical thinking does not necessarily mean emotional problems. What counts is whether such thinking interferes with everyday functioning.

We should not be at the skeptic end of the spectrum, anyway. To be totally non-magical is very unhealthy, says Peter Burgger, head of neuropsychology at University Hospital, Zurich. He has data, for example, strongly linking lack of magical ideation to anhedonia, which is the inability to experience pleasure. Students who are not magical do not typically enjoy going to parties. There is a key chemical involved in magical thinking -- Dopamine, the neurotransmitter the brain uses to make experiences meaningful. It floods the brains of schizophrenics, who see significance in everything, but there is very little in the brain of a depressed person, who struggles to find value in everyday life.

Finally, Arthur C. Clarke's assertion that any sufficiently advanced technology is indistinguishable from magic, comes to full fruition in cyberspace, the realm of avatars and instant messaging. As magical thinking may help us pluck the fruits of digital technology, it is not so silly after all.

Chapter Nineteen

The Energy of Thoughts

Everything is energy and that is all there is to it.
Match the frequency of the reality you want and you cannot
help but get that reality. It can be no other way.
This is not philosophy. This is physics. -- Albert Einstein

Your thoughts are the currencies with which you exchange energy with the universe. Positive thought, energy in the form of collective meditation, has been scientifically proven to reduce violent crime. In 1993 a study by Dr. Jeffrey R. Palmer, one of the world's leading physicists, undertook an experiment in Washington D.C. to determine if focused meditation could have an effect on New York City's crime rate. The results were astonishing. Several volunteers mediated, and the crime rate fell by 25%. Because all life is a bundle of energy, and we tend to influence each other profoundly.

Negative thoughts create negative events, positive thoughts create positive results. Every thought interacts with the energy of the universe; negative thought looks for other negative thought energy to bind with. Eventually a matrix of negative thought energy is created and forms a thought wave. These powerful negative thought waves manifest themselves in our lives in the form of poverty, crime, war, plagues, and natural disasters. Positive thought energy creates surpluses; it is the surpluses of positive thought energy that allow for the abundance in life.

Consciousness at its deepest level is a field that underlies and connects individuals throughout society. Carl Jung has talked about the archetypes we inherited from our ancestors, both bad and good, even though our mind tends to keep flirting with the negative ones. Quantum physics shows how

116

thoughts can play major roles in producing unintended consequences. The law of attraction is the best example of that, discussed in another chapter of this book.

What the bleep do we know? A fascinating experiment was conducted by Dr. Masaru Emoto, a Japanese scientist who investigated the effect of positive words on water. He measured how thought and feeling can affect water, or the physical reality of water. When he focused intention through written and spoken words and music, and presented it to a water sample, the water appeared to change its expression. He found that water from clear springs and water which had been exposed to loving words showed brilliant, complex, and colorful snowflake patterns. In contrast, polluted water, or water exposed to negative thoughts formed incomplete, asymmetrical patterns with dull color. The implication of this research has created a new awareness of how we can positively or negatively impact the earth, personal health, and surroundings.

If thoughts can do this to water, imagine what they can do to us! Our bodies are primarily made of water, approximately 70%. If positive emotions, words, and feelings can change the physical structure of water, that means self-talk has a direct effect on the biology of our being. If you knew how powerful your thoughts were, you would never think a bad thought, which can fire and wire the synapses of your brain, and become part of who you are. So the next time you are feeling a negative emotion, or feeling negative thoughts, remember that you are a having physical impact on your biological system. Your cells, and everything that makes up your physical body, is always responding to you. So be good to yourself, and give yourself loving thoughts, because, they will be manifested all over your body and the surrounding space.

Thought is a living dynamic force; you can pollute the world with negative thoughts. The mind is like land fertile for planting; you have to plow it and remove the weeds. If you do not tend it daily, the weeds will grow. It is the same with the mind too. Keep it clean by removing your mind's dross, because a serene mind is a valuable spiritual asset for you. Austerity of speech keeps the mind calm, and saturates your mind with thoughts of love and peace.

Are thought processes influenced by body position? Dr. Hugo C. Beigel of Long Island University showed that when you recline, your thinking is more complacent, you tend to have more association, and let your mind range wide for ideas. In a standing position, your energy is stimulated toward action, the thinking field is narrowed, the influx of new suggestions is partly blocked, and decisions come faster and are more vigorous. Sitting seems a compromise between the opposing tendencies of standing and lying down.

Most people have it backward, believing they feel or think a certain way because of their circumstances, not knowing it is their thought power creating those very circumstances, wanted or unwanted.

Your thoughts are alive. The greatest mystics and teachers to walk the earth have told us that everything is energy, as Albert Einstein indicated. William Walker told us, "where the mind is static energy, thought is dynamic energy." Charles Haanel went on to say that "thought power is the vibratory force formed by converting the static mind into the dynamic mind." The subconscious mind is the storehouse of your deep seated beliefs and programs. We have to re-program, because we can use the power of our thoughts to change our life and circumstances.

Mental telepathy is another amazing energy our thoughts can have. The term comes from the ancient Greek; *tele* means distant, and *pathos* or *patheia* meaning feeling, perception, passion. It also means the transmission of information from one person to another without using any sensory channels or physical interaction. As we know, thought has energy, so this implies that two people are able to share their thoughts with each other without the intervention of the five senses.

Have you ever experienced the situation where you thought of someone, then suddenly found him calling you, or next to you on the train? Have you ever felt worried about someone, then suddenly get a phone call stating that person had an accident? Have you ever thought of someone you have not seen for years, then suddenly ran into him? What is that all about? It is telepathy, a thought which seems to be a form of communication between minds; when a person thinks about something and the other person receives that thought, we call it mental telepathy.

Does it really exist? People are divided into two groups; some deny its existence, while others believe in it. Some experiments were done to prove that telepathy exists, but the non-believers questioned the methodology used in these experiments. In order for telepathy to be accepted by science, researchers must be able to reproduce results under scientifically controlled situations. To date, that has not been done. Personally, I do believe in telepathy, because I have had several situations that I have no way to explain, other than through mental telepathy.

Why does telepathy exist? When God created this ultimate creature called man, He gave him tremendous powers, but these powers were lost because of lack of practice. For example, your mind can make very complex calculations without using a calculator, but the reason you now run to a calculator when you want to know the product of something as simple as 57 x 18, is lack of practice. Therefore, technology has taught us how to be lazy; the more we use technology the more we bury some of our abilities like telepathy. Moreover, some people have a better telepathic ability than others; those are the overly sensitive people, who have high empathic tendencies which help process telepathy.

A double-blind experiment confirmed the existence of *psi*, or psychic power, but what is the physical process by which mental telepathy operates? Recent discoveries in quantum physics (the study of the physics of sub-atomic particles) and in cosmology shed some light on how the mind interacts with the universe. The discovery compels acceptance of the idea that there is far more than just one universe, and we constantly interact with many of these hidden universes.

As Albert Einstein said, imagination is everything; it is the preview of life's coming attractions. Thoughts create everything, but here is the problem. Most people spend their time thinking about what they do not want, and wondering why it shows up over and over again. When people think, speak, act, and focus on what they do not want, they keep it alive, and it will show up.

You can free yourself from this "do not want" epidemic by thinking and speaking about what you want. Your thoughts not only matter, they create matter. Thought is where everything comes from. Consciousness is what the universe is made of. Matter and energy are just two of the forms that consciousness takes. Everything is made of thoughts, and thoughts create the physical world.

Therefore, the conclusions are: 1) Everything in the physical world is made of atoms; 2) Atoms are created by energy; 3) Energy is made through consciousness. Capture this concept; it is fundamental to our realization that thoughts have energy and can harm or heal us. Throughout this book, you have seen how the power of thoughts can shape your life.

The truth is, we do not see what is there, we see what we are prepared to see, or what we are conditioned to see. You have heard the old expression, "I'll believe it when I see it," but that's not really how it is. The truth is more "you will see it when you believe it."

In a very real concrete sense, your beliefs do not simply reflect your reality; they create it. Listen to your thoughts. What are the dominant thoughts that run through your mind? We often think of our body and mind as two distinct entities, but it turns out they are much more entwined than we assumed. Researchers are continually finding evidence that the brain has distinct power to manipulate the body's physiology. There are few examples of how the energy of our thoughts can change the physical reality, but there are numerous examples of how our thoughts can actually alter our physical world or reality:

1) Drying Sheets. Tibetan monks have better control over mind and body than the average person. They meditate for hours, abstain from food for days, and take a vow of silence. They control physiological processes, such as blood pressure and body temperature, astounding the rest of us. In one notable experiment, a group of Tibetan monks engaged in Yoga and meditation (they call it *gTummo*). During this process the monks were covered by wet sheets, and placed in a 40f (4.5c) room. In such conditions the average person would likely experience uncontrollable shivering and shortly suffer hypothermia. But, through deep concentration, the monks were able to generate body heat and within minutes the researchers noticed steam rising from the sheets that were covering the monks. Within an hour the sheets were completely dry. The monks generated enough heat or energy to reach a state of altered reality, a place unaffected by our everyday world.

2) Multiple Personality Disorder, or dissociative identity disorder, is a mental condition, perhaps the most intriguing of all of them. We see the energy of thoughts work, because personality and behavior change as someone switches among different personalities. We see measurable physiological variations between each persona. For example, one of them might wear eyeglasses and the another one does not.. Or one identity might be diabetic and the other one is in perfect health. In such cases, it is not simply a matter of the patients thinking they need eyeglasses or insulin. Their bodies actually go through legitimate alteration in vision or blood sugar level.

There are several cases published by the American Psychiatric Press regarding how medication prescribed to a dissociative identity disorder patient had different effects, depending on what personality took the drugs. For example, when a tranquilizer was given to the person with a childish persona, it made him sleepy and relaxed, while if the same medication was administered to an adult personality, it made him anxious and confused. Similar results are found with other patients and different medications. This phenomenon is fascinating. No one claims mysticism as a cause; on the contrary, it is a genuine example of how the mind alters the body.

I saw one patient in my clinic in Michigan who switched her personality two to three times. She reported to me that she had been in a serious trauma, and uses these personalities as a coping mechanism. One personality is dumb, and does not know simple things, and the other one is very bright and can pass exams without difficulty.

3) The Placebo Effect. A placebo is an inert substance which produces real biological effects. It is widely accepted as fact that a placebo variable is included in most medical tests as a way of proving a drug works on its own merits, or because people think it works. There are thousands of experiments showing the proof of the placebo, but there is one amazing experiment done by a group of Princeton University students who decided to throw a non-alcoholic party for their unsuspecting classmates. The experimenters secretly filled a keg with O'Doul's, which contains about 0.4% alcohol, (regular beer has around 5%) and then watched as their peers acted silly, slurred words, slept on the ground, and generally acted drunk. Although it is nearly impossible to get intoxicated on O'Doul's, these college students had such a strong belief they were drinking standard beer that it affected their behavior.

4) The Nocebo Effect. While placebos are generally associated with positive outcomes, like curing an illness or getting "drunk" on O'Doul's and having fun (if you consider that positive), the nocebo effect produces negative results, such as cancer patients vomiting before chemotherapy starts, or breaking out in a rash because they thought they touched poison ivy, even though they were merely maple leaves.

One of the most well-known examples of the nocebo phenomenon was an incident published in the *New Science Journal*. According to the account, late one night an Alabama man called Vance went to a cemetery and met with a witch doctor who told Vance that he was going to die soon. Vance believed the witch doctor's prediction, fell ill, and within a matter of weeks was emaciated and close to death. Vance was taken to the hospital, but the medical doctor found nothing wrong with him.

Finally, Vance's wife told Dr. Doherthy about his encounter with the witch doctor, which gave the creative Dr. Doherthy an idea. The next day, Dr. Doherthy told the couple she had tracked down the witch doctor and physically threatened him until the medicine man finally admitted he had put a lizard inside Vance that was eating him from the inside. Of course, the doctor's story was completely fabricated, yet she made a big show of injecting the patient with a mysterious substance and snuck in a genuine green lizard that she pretended to extract from Vance. The next day, Vance awoke alert, hungry, and it did not take long before he fully recovered. This story was corroborated by four other medical professionals, and often cited when explaining why Voodoo sometimes works -- because of the nocebo effect.

5) Dreams can cause real injuries. There are a lot of stories floating around about people who experience something in their dreams and then found real physical evidence of wounds on their bodies once they awake. People claim being attacked during a dream and wake up to find scratch marks on their bodies. There is well-documented case reported by well-known psychiatrist Ian Stevenson, about an Indian man named Durga Jatav. During a battle with typhoid fever, he had an extremely vivid dream that captors cut his legs off at the knee. Unfortunately, his legs were already severed by the time the captors realized they had the wrong man and did not need to keep Durga after all. When Durga asked how he could leave with no legs, they offered him several pairs of legs, he picked out his own, and then they were miraculously reattached.

While Durga was having the dream, his body became very cold and at one point his family thought he was dead, yet he revived a few days later. Once he was awake his sister and neighbor noticed deep fissures around his knee that were previously not there. X-rays showed no abnormality below the surface of the skin, which led Durga's family to believe the marks came from his dream experience. Dr. Stevenson met Durga some 30 years later in 1979, and took pictures of the still visible scars. Dr. Stevenson did not see the story, but it was confirmed by all of the people involved. He reported the account of story in his book *Reincarnation and Biology*.

Perhaps these stories can contribute to the etiology of birthmarks and birth defects. Obviously, there is not scientific proof of this intriguing account, but it is not too far-fetched, considering what we already know about the power of the brain over body and our surroundings, and the energy of thoughts.

6) There were Indian yogis who had an unusual talent for manipulating their physiological processes while in deep meditation. After hearing the stories of yogis spending 28 days underground and surviving, in 1936, a French cardiologist named Therese Brosse traveled to India to see if the yogis truly did have such a talent In her experiment, the yogis slowed their hearts down so slow that a heartbeat was only detectable via an EKG.

In 1950, Brosse's study was expanded by another group of researchers who traveled to India with an eight channel electro-encephalograph and various other instruments, which they used to monitor the yogis' brain activity, respiration, skin temperature, blood volume changes and skin conductance. Two of their test subjects were placed in air-tight sealed boxes, on two separate occasions, and were monitored for 8 to 10 hours. During that time, the yogis showed biological characteristics similar to sleep, and were able to slow down their heart rate and respiration to a low enough level that oxygen and carbon dioxide quantities inside the box remained virtually in the same proportion as found in the air at sea level. Thus, they slowed down their body processes and did not panic, which most of us would do. Thus, yogis could survive a live burial for far longer than the average person.

7) Positivity and Meditation: Recently, David Seidler, who wrote *The King's Speech*, claimed to have eliminated his cancer through meditation and imagination. After a battle with bladder cancer for several years and only two weeks from surgery, David decided to see if he could get rid of the cancer through his imagination. So in the two weeks leading up to surgery, he envisioned a clean, cream-colored, healthy bladder. When David went to his pre-surgery biopsy, the doctor was astounded to find a distinct lack of cancer, even after repeating the biopsy at four different testing labs. He attributed no trace of cancer to his visualization; his doctor called it spontaneous remission.

8) The energy of the thought of gaining weight is becoming an epidemic worldwide, and it seems nothing works. But Dr. Ellen Langer thought that

what is missing in the equation is the power, or the energy, of positive thought. So she conducted an experiment on a group of predominately overweight hotel maids. Judging them by their daily activity level, they should have been thin. Despite essential exercise all day long through their work, Langer discovered through a survey that 67% of the maids do not do any type of exercise.

Langer postulated that the maids' perception was hampering their weight loss. She took half the maids aside, and in addition to taking their physical measurement, explained to them that through their cleaning work they were exceeding the surgeon general's definition of an active lifestyle. The other half of the maids were given no information. A month later, Langer's team returned to the hotel and reevaluated the maids. They found an overall decrease in systolic blood pressure, weight, and waist-to-hip ratio in the informed group. The other group had no significant physical changes. Some suspected the mere discussion of exercise somehow altered the women's behavior. There is no indication that those maids changed or modified their daily routine; rather, the changes could be the result of changing their mindset by changing their perceptions about their bodies. Undoubtedly, that is the power or energy of our thoughts. If we use it effectively it can alter body weight.

If we look closely at the epidemic of weight gain around the world, and the enormous programs for weight reduction, the result is shameful. The message here is wrong. People focus on reducing weight, and hating their bodies. Thus, the body will not give in and lose the weight. If you really want to lose weight you have to love your body and not focus on losing weight, because we just have learned in a previous chapter that what you resist, will persist. The best approach to losing weight is to focus your energy on having a healthy lifestyle and cherishing your body. Without hesitation, I can assure you, you will lose weight.

Chapter Twenty

The Child Riding an Elephant

Metaphorically speaking, our life is like a child riding an elephant. Normally, the child has no control over the elephant, and the elephant is wandering around aimlessly. The child looks helpless, scared, frightened, anxious, and occasionally amazed. The child is us, and the elephant is our unconsciousness, which controls 90% of our daily activities.

So then, what is the nature of consciousness? It is merely a by-product of the physical brain. Nevertheless, consciousness is perhaps the greatest mystery ever presented to mankind.

The unconscious mind hijacks our personality. Each of us has a unique set of experiences, and it is within these life experiences that we develop beliefs, values, and perceptions. Often, these beliefs are limited, irrational, and faulty in nature. How we perceive the world, and how we derive meaning from each situation, is filtered through our limited belief system. When we function this way, we are in the ego-state, and able to see only a distorted and filtered truth.

For example, a man's partner respectfully disagrees about the way he handled a situation with a co-worker. The man feels threatened, defensive, and angry and lashes out at the partner for not taking his side and not understanding him. He begins to take the disagreement personally and through his arrested limited belief, he becomes what was ingrained in his consciousness since childhood. That triggers his unconscious mind to hijack the conscious mind, because it reverts back to a childlike state. In this example, perhaps, as a child, he felt he was not important, or heard, or valued as a person. Now, in adult life, if ever involved in a disagreement, his beliefs of feeling unheard and unimportant are triggered without his awareness.

Out false limiting beliefs are irrational and sit in our unconscious mind like land mines waiting to be stepped on. After they are triggered, if we never attempt to understand or process them, they patiently wait for another experience to ignite them. Each of us walks around with a filter holding false beliefs created in our childhood. We let our experiences pass through this filter. When we begin to understand what our filters are, we become more aware of our triggers and the story we've been telling ourselves. As children, we did not have a choice of a knowledge base, and we accepted what we were shown. As adults, we have a choice to unlearn and learn.

Thus, as an adult we must learn mindfulness techniques to allow us o stay in the moment and process what we are experiencing, rather than being hijacked by the elephant. This technique is similar to the refresh button on an internet page-each moment is new. Mindfulness is seeing everything just as it is without interpretation.. Diaphragmatic breathing can help us return to the moment, to slow the nervous system down, and regain mental balance and physical clarity (Kristi A. De Name).

The unconscious mind is responsible for 90% of our decision making. We do not always actively notice it, but it is the part of our mind that is always assessing the situation and matching it with early relationships and experiences. There is a constant negotiation between our conscious and unconscious mind when you are faced with certain circumstances; often the unconscious takes over; that is the elephant.

Imagine you are on your way to a job interview. You are nervous, you do not feel that you measure up, so you unconsciously miss the exit on the highway and show up late. You have actively not measured up, jeopardizing your chance at the job. Your unconscious feeling was close enough to the surface of your conscious mind to influence your actions. Thus, the unconscious mind is in hijack mode to change the direction of what we consciously set out to do. Another common hijack example is a slip of the tongue, commonly known as the Freudian slip.

Today's technology has created an entirely new platform for unconscious miscommunication to play out in our everyday lives. Tech-based communications are devoid of any emotion and tone, yet we read intent and meaning into them. Both your mental and physical health depend on understanding that the conscious and unconscious are linked, and communicate with each other all the time. Being mindful of that link will help you learn more about your authentic self, and better notice the communication that passes between those sectors of the mind. Once you become more effective at redirecting a potential inner hijack into a co-pilot, you will start to have a healthier outlook and notice lasting change.

Thus, our life is a reflection of our unconscious programming, because the job of the unconscious is to create reality out of its own program, and try to prove that program is true. If you have negative programs in your unconscious, Dr. Bruce Lipton says 95% of the time those negative experiences will be recreated in your life. Those of us who have ever taken the time to check out unconscious thoughts know that most of the programs of the unconscious mind are based in negativity and fear of not being loved.

Why is our unconscious mind running our life? The answer has been introduced by Dr. Bruce Lipton, molecular biologist, who says the new science of epigenetics has shown that our genes are in fact controlled and manipulated by how our mind perceives and interprets our environment. Formerly, science believed it was the genes themselves that dictated our traits. This new finding is great news, because it means we can change many things about the way we are, including our health, by changing how we interpret events and situations.

Lipton shows if we interpret things in a positive way, we start living healthier and better quality lives, regardless of the genetic makeup we started with. A new attitude, positive or negative, sends new messages to the cells in our body, and can actually reprogram their health and behavior. It can even change cellular structure, turning diseased cells into healthy cells. Two separate minds create what he calls the body controlling voice: the conscious mind, which can think freely and create new ideas, and the unconscious mind, which is basically a super computer loaded with a database of programming behaviors, most of which we acquired before we reached age six.

The unconscious mind cannot move outside of its fixed programs. It automatically reacts to situations with its previously stored behavior response. And, it works without the knowledge or control of the conscious mind. This is why we are generally unaware of our behavior; in fact, most of the time we are not even aware that we are acting unconsciously. Our brain begins to prepare for action just over a third of a second before we consciously decide to act. In other words, even when we think we are conscious, it is our unconscious mind which is actually making our decisions for us. The unconscious mind is running us on automatic pilot 95% of the time.

Neuroscientists have shown that the conscious mind provides 5% or less of our cognitive conscious activity during the day Many people operate at just 1% consciousness. Dr. Lipton says that the unconscious mind operates at 40 million bits of data per second. So the unconscious mind is much more powerful than the conscious mind, and tends to shape how we live life. Scientists have shown that most of our decisions, actions, emotions, and behaviors depend on the 95% of brain activity that is beyond our conscious awareness, which means that 95-99% of our life comes from the programming in our unconscious mind.

Carl Jung said primitive man went to great lengths to describe all he saw or experienced. Thus, Jung believed that events of nature were not simply put into fairy tales and myths as a way of explaining them physically. Rather, the outer world was used to make sense of the inner world. In our time, Jung noted this rich well of symbols, art, religion, and mythology, which for thousands of years helped people understand the mysteries of life, has been filled in and replaced by the science of psychology.

For Jung, the goal of life was to see the individuation of the self, a sort of uniting of a person's conscious and unconscious mind, so that their original unique promise might be fulfilled. While Freud assumed the unconscious to be a personal thing contained within an individual, Jung, on the other hand, saw the personal unconscious mind as sitting atop a much deeper universal layer of consciousness, the collective unconsciousness, the inherited part of the human psyche not developed from personal experiences.

The collective unconsciousness was expressed through archetypes; these universal thoughts form our mental images that influence an individual's feelings and actions. The experiences of archetypes often paid little heed to tradition or cultural rules, which suggests they are innate projections. A newborn is not a blank slate, but comes wired ready to perceive certain archetypal patterns and symbols. This is why children fantasize so much, according to Jung; they have not experienced enough of reality to control out their mind's enjoyment of archetypal imagery. Jung also noted that in evolutionary terms, the unconscious comes well before the development of conscious thought. Yet in its youthful enthusiasm, the conscious mind feels it can defy or deny it deeper counterpart.

While the unconscious seems a murky irrelevance, Jung believed man's worst sin is the unconscious. We project everything we do not like or cannot accept internally onto the world, so that we wage war instead of studying ourselves. It is a case of anything but self-knowledge, and in the end we pay the price, whether as an individual or collectively. Jung summed it up when he said, "There are certain events of which we have not consciously taken note; they have remained, so to speak, below the threshold of the conscious. They have happened, but they have been observed subliminally."

Jung focused on the spiritual aspect of the unconscious mind. For example Winston Churchill reported to have heard a voice saying stop, just before he was about to enter his car. A second later, a bomb exploded, which most likely would have killed him had he been inside his vehicle. Such examples show how powerful the unconscious part of our mind can be, and suggests that we are connected to a higher power or force that can guide us along our path in life, if only we are aware of it and tap into it. Perhaps it is a spiritual power, not a materialistic one.

What are the secrets of our the unconscious mind? We exert some power over our thoughts by directing our attention, like a spotlight to focus on something specific. The consequences of doing so can be amusing, as in the famous experiment in which about a third of the people watching a basketball game failed to spot a man in a gorilla suit crossing the court. Or, the consequences can be disastrous, as when a narrow focus prevents a driver from noticing a light turning red or an oncoming train.

Joseph Murphy has theorized we do not realize our potential, because our unconscious mind does not know what is real and what is imagined. Under this we see the law of attraction. How can we use it for our benefit? As Thomas Miller said, the unconscious is as miraculous component of human anatomy as are our brain, heart, lungs, or any other component of our incredible physiology.

People often ask how the unconscious mind impacts our behavior. Not all actions are a result of our conscious decisions; most of our actions are the result of what Perm Kamble calls Mental Reflex Actions, over which we have little control. We are not in control of the actions governed by our unconscious mind. We are aware of only tiny little things that go on in our mind, and we can control only a tiny part of our conscious thoughts. The vast majority of our thinking efforts go on unconsciously. Only one or two of these thoughts are likely to break into consciousness at a time.

Slips of the tongue and accidental actions offer glimpses of our unfiltered unconscious mental life. The intrusive thoughts you may experience throughout the day illustrate the disconcerting fact that many of the functions of the mind are outside of our conscious control. Whether we maintain true control over any mental functions is the central debate about free will. Perhaps this lack of autonomy is to be expected as the foundation for almost all the mind's labors were laid long before our ancestors evolved consciousness. Even deliberate decisions are not completely under our power. Our awareness only sets the start and end of a goal, but leaves the implementation to unconscious mental processes.

Fay Thompson said our mind contains the whole history from every lifetime, and always gravitates to what is known, not what is best for you. The unknown is scary to the unconscious mind, because it cannot calculate a known outcome with an unknown variable. This is why people tend to repeat thoughts and behaviors they know. They will stay in the same abusive relationship, or always go down a familiar path. Because it is what they know and their mind understands the outcome. Michael Craig brings a fresh perspective, saying we learn between birth and 7 years unconsciously. For example, we learn our mother tongue, and that is why we never forget our mother tongue, and speak it so fluently and effortlessly. It was learned unconsciously.

Dr. Lipton compared the unconscious to a tape recorder; it does not judge or analyze, it just tapes things as they are. The same process is true for the unconscious mind. It does not judge, or analyze or make any difference between right and wrong or good or bad. For example if a woman learned unconsciously that men beat women, because she was beaten by her father or grew up observing her father beating her mother, this could become her unconscious programming regarding men's behavior toward women.

Consciously, she would never choose a man based on this negative quality, but because this is normal as per her unconscious programming, she would most likely end up with a man who mistreats her. This is a situation we find in most cases of battered women. Here we can see how the child rides an elephant, as we are somehow unable to have access to the unconscious mind. In order to break away from such cycles, she needs to reprogram her unconscious mind, because, the conscious has the will, while the unconscious has the power.

Chapter Twenty-One

The Role of Psychology in Correcting Erroneous Thoughts

A great percentage of our available mental energy is used up in unconscious conflict, and not enough is left to provide the normal enjoyment of life and vitality. Thus, psychology deals with unconscious conflict.

Problems cannot be solved at the same level of thinking that created them, (Albert Einstein). Therefore psychology comes to provide another level of thinking and understanding to human behavior.

All of our behaviors result from thoughts that preceded them, so the thing to work on is not your behavior but the thing that caused your behavior, and that is your thoughts (Wayne Dyer). Psychology teaches people therapeutic skills of how to arrest disturbing thoughts, thus making their lives more enjoyable and meaningful. Ultimately, that is what we dream to have.

What do we mean by erroneous thoughts? It's thinking that plagues most of our life. We are trapped in a vicious cycle of negative thinking, causing enjoyment to be remote from us. We are plagued by guilt and worry, and we find ourselves unwittingly falling into the same old self-destructive patterns. In fact, our approach to life can become a barrier to success and happiness. Unfortunately, we believe that we have no control over our life, a feather in the wind of life flying aimlessly. It is that way because we let people and events affect our life, and we do not have the skills to manage difficult times. We do not have an understanding of the nature of our dysfunctional thoughts.

One of the prevailing errors in our thinking is that we spend too much time worrying over what others may think, instead of working on what we want and need. You will always be disappointed because you leave your assessment of yourself to other people. If caught up in old labels and an out-of-date self-image, you conceal great potential. How can you break away and fulfill your desires for what you want to be? If you depend on people for fulfillment, you will never be fulfilled.

At birth, programming starts to take place within us, until we establish a paradigm that will direct us for the rest of our lives. The programming is very powerful until age six, because our brain in this stage is very vulnerable.

Ask yourself, am I happy? If the answer is no, then you owe it to yourself to find and investigate the source of your unhappiness. Identify the thinking that blocks you from being happy. Then you have to take serious steps to change and make your life a happy one. Life is a risk; we are all going to die, so why not do what we want with our lives? We are not happy because there are errors in our thinking, or the way we approach life. The focus of this chapter is how to correct our thinking patterns.

Another common erroneous thought is we think life should be fair; it will never be. Injustice has prevailed since God kicked us from Eden. Thus, we must take life wholesale; we cannot pick and choose. Once you look for images of justice, you will become incapacitated with anger, guilt, worry, or indignation. Life's circumstances will never change. We are up against impossible odds.

Once we identify erroneous thinking and maladaptive behavior, we are able to use psychological interventions suitable for each psychological difficulty. Normally, we learn faulty thinking in the early years of life, but there are thinking traps involved in day to day transactions. For example, we may jump to conclusions, or have prior assumptions about a person or a situation.

Another pattern of erroneous thinking is cognitive distortion. It is an exaggerated or irrational thought pattern believed to perpetuate the effects of a psychopathological state, or it is thoughts that make an individual perceive reality inaccurately. These thinking patterns often reinforce negative thoughts and emotions, as well as negative personal views toward the world. Consequently, we become depressed or anxious, or out of balance mentally. Another faulty thinking trap is making a mountain out of a molehill, or exaggeration, and magnifications. This pattern of thinking is another component of erroneous thinking, which takes a toll on an individual.

Catastrophic thinking and over-generalization are fueled by emotion. Faulty thinking is devious, because it usually occurs on the unconscious level. In narrative therapy, we often discuss what the dominant story is about you, created by others in your life, and that it probably does not reflect who you really are. Catastrophic thinking is the tendency to assume the worst and spend much of our time thinking and planning to face the worst. This type of thinking tends to increase anxiety, and makes life a gloomy trip.

Confirmation bias, which is the acceptance of only information and data that supports your current beliefs and values, is another form of faulty thinking. This is the classic "do not bother me with the facts" stance. You do not have to look very far to find this type of thinking; it is rampant in any society. There is also black or white thinking, where there is no gray area, no flexibility. Such thinking encourages rigidity, not resilience. We are irrational beings, loaded with pathology, and a lot of ridiculous things which have brought us pain and misery. We are living it, and it seems we are unable to discharge ourselves from such dysfunctional lives.

The art of being miserable. Most people claim or declare they want to be happy, to have a meaningful life, enjoy themselves, experience fulfillment, and share love and friendship with other people. Strangely enough, that is not true in most cases. On the contrary, most people unconsciously want to be miserable, and they succeed remarkably at inviting misery into their lives.

Why do they do that? After being in the field of treatment and psychology for more than 30 years, I started to understand the dynamics of the human mind, and that being miserable is an art form. The satisfaction people seem to find in it reflects the creative effort required to cultivate it. In other words, when your living conditions are stable, peaceful, and prosperous, you do not have the challenge of struggling hard in life. Making yourself miserable is a craft all its own, requiring imagination, vision, and ingenuity. It can even give life a distinctive meaning.

Being miserable may give you pleasure, so you cannot be disappointed or disillusioned about life's circumstances. Being miserable can give the impression you are a wise and worldly person, especially if you are miserable not just about your life, but about society in general. You project an aura of someone burdened by a form of profound tragic, existential knowledge that happy, shallow people cannot possibly appreciate (Cole Madane).

Making ourselves follow a set of rules that leads to misery can be an unconscious process. If everyone is pursuing happiness and you are pursuing misery, you become a distinct and unique individual; you become one of a kind. You might be attracting the wrong kind of attention, but you will be attracting attention. Some people will hold you up as an example of what not to do, but they will talk about you; they will be interested.

The first step in psychological change is to identify the maladaptive thoughts which block you from the happy life that you would like to have. Once we do that, then we may go to the next step, which is the methods we use to challenge those thoughts. Socrates used questioning to encourage his students to arrive at the answer they sought. Instead of simply responding to students' questions or providing lectures, he systematically asked questions that encouraged deep thought, which allowed students to gain knowledge through critical thinking. This is called the Socratic Method. Cognitive therapists often use the Socratic Method to help people challenge maladaptive, unrealistic and unbalanced thoughts. We can learn to challenge our own thoughts through the Socratic Method as well.

Cognitive distortion is a distorted pattern of thought. There are myriad kinds of distortion, like catastrophizing, labeling, discounting positive thoughts, negative filtering, overgeneralization, personalization, blaming, and unfair comparison. All these emotional reasonings skew your interpretation of the reality. For example, I feel depressed, therefore my marriage is not working. I feel anxious, therefore I must be in danger. In such cases, dysfunctional behavior tends to prevail, and erroneous thoughts take deeper roots in our unconscious mind.

We surround ourselves with information that matches our beliefs. We tend to like people who like us or think like us. Unconsciously, we begin to ignore or dismiss anything that threatens our world view; this is called confirmation bias. Another concept is called frequency illusion, which is similar. When you buy a car, you suddenly see the same car everywhere; if you are pregnant, you suddenly notice other pregnant women.

David McRanoy said "wherever your opinion or beliefs are so intertwined with your self-image, you cannot pull them away without damaging your core concept of self. You avoid situations which may cause harm to those beliefs." What a profound concept therapists must tackle. When we see a patient's self-concept wrapped up with certain beliefs, that makes his or her life emotionally unbearable.

We worry over things already lost; we are wired to feel loss far stronger than gain. Unfortunately, we focus on the loss more than the gain. We incorrectly predict the odds that there is a glitch in our thinking, and that proves us to be illogical creatures. We rationalize purchases we do not want; we are pretty good at convincing ourselves that such purchases are necessary. This is post-purchase rationalization.

Cognitive dissonance is the discomfort we get when we try to hold onto competing ideas or theories. Often, we believe our memories more than facts; the memory is highly fallible and plastic, yet we tend to unconsciously favor it over objective facts. We pay more attention to stereotypes than we think, related to a memory that is so ingrained we easily ignore actual facts. The human mind is so wedded to stereotypes and so distracted by vivid description that it will seize upon them, even when they defy logic, rather than rely upon relevant facts.

Dr. Athena Staik writes that habitual thinking patterns which cause intense feelings of fear, anger, shame, or guilt, are not only toxic, but also addictive. They stimulate the pleasure and learning centers of the brain, similar to addictive substances. Toxic thinking is characteristically compulsive and causes intense fear-based feelings, which can overwhelm and sap our body's energy. It consists of thoughts that habitually forecast disaster, perpetuate worry, instill doubt, obsess on perfection, and paint you as a victim. So how can these painful feelings stimulate pleasure?

Toxic thoughts paint an image of the self and others with gloom or failure. However unconsciously, they are protective strategies that get activated automatically as a defense when something triggers them. Thus, our body associates them with pseudo good feelings that lower our anxiety, albeit briefly, but it is a quick fix. Toxic thoughts stimulate the reward center of the brain, and the mixed emotions of pleasure and fear stimulate these centers to establish an addiction. Addictive relating patterns, or emotional reactivity in general, produce dopamine, a neurotransmitter, a chemical messenger of the brain that plays a major role in forming addictions, and habits in general, healthy or otherwise. It transmits teaching signals to the reward center of the brain responsible for acquiring new habits.

Fear also can stimulate the reward center for the release of hormones. Fear works together with pleasure to enhance and intensify the "high" in the reward center. In fact, the brain is at its most receptivity to learning in the presence of danger. Fear not only reinforces learning, it also increases the chance that a particular memory will receive preferential attention from the unconscious mind. This means the unconscious mind will record the experiences in a special place in the memory, an intelligence report of sorts, which the unconscious mind turns to whenever we feel threatened.

Toxic thinking patterns act as drugs of choice; fear pushes us to the fight or flee response and activates powerful inner processes which produce dynamic physiological changes in the body automatically. They disengage the higher thinking processes of the brain. As a result, our brain goes into learning or protective mode.

The individual Arab brain is mostly in protective mode, with the thriving mode shut off. Thus we do not see any development in the Arab world, because individual Arabs most of the time are trying to manage their protective mode. There is a lot of transgression on most areas of individual lives. Thus, there is no time or energy left for the thriving brain. Because of consistent abuse and disappointment, Arab individuals do not thrive or excel.

Our brain is wired to produce a constant learning; all learning generates change in the brain. When you seek to replace a behavior, such as toxic thinking patterns, actions produce neurochemical and molecular changes in cells. As neurons communicate with each other by transmitting electrical signals between them, these signals are activated by the exchange of chemicals in the synapses. Our brain and body are sophisticated communication networks. Your unconscious mind manages all of the systemic processes you do not have to think about, as well as all of your personal requests, wants or commands, both conscious and unconscious. The vast and complex networks manage the flow of information that shapes behavior in many facets of life. These electrical impulses are "molecules of emotion" designed to control the overall direction of your life.

Psychology, as a science and profession, has contributed to the wellbeing of humanity as well as freeing people from their erroneous thinking. The study of human life has become a great discipline over the past quarter century, extending across substantive and diverse boundaries in social and behavioral science. Psychology took so long to emerge as a scientific discipline because it needed time to consolidate the understanding of human behavior, thoughts and feelings. That is not easy, which may explain why it was largely ignored from the ancient Greek era to the 16th century. There are several psychological approaches that can restore the correct the pattern of thinking, to make the life of an individual less troubling:

1) Psychoanalysis is the oldest approach, which has a great explanatory power and understanding of behavior. But it has been accused of only explaining behavior after the event, not predicting what will happen in advance, and of being un-falsifiable. Kline (1984) argues that psychology theory can be broken down into testable hypotheses and tested scientifically. For example, Scodol (1957), postulated that orally dependent men prefer large breasted women; a positive correlation, and found the opposite a negative correlation. Freud has contributed immensely to the field of psychology and understanding the dynamic of thinking, through reaction formation, in which the subject shows exactly the opposite of their unconscious impulses.

Understanding the problem is half of the solution. Thus psychoanalysis focuses on making unconscious materials conscious, so an individual becomes aware of hidden materials. Once aware, the individual can change them, or choose not to reinforce them. Psychoanalysis explains the nature of anxiety, depression, phobias, panic, and other thought disorders, as well as provides us with keen observations of human behavior, and a great defense mechanism to manage anxiety.

2) Behaviorism uses a few simple principles (reinforcement, behavior shaping, generalization, etc.) to explain a vast variety of behavior, from language acquisition to moral development. Thorndike's Law of Affect possesses a core of determinism from the environment. Behaviorism firmly believes in the scientific principle of determinism and orderliness, and comes up with fairly consistent predictions of when an animal is likely to respond, and uses such predictions to control the behavior of both animals and humans. Skinner described a society controlled according to behavior principles.

3) Cognitive Therapy identifies maladaptive beliefs, and achieves self-actualization to empower the patient. Now called Cognitive Behavioral Therapy, it can be used to treat people with a wide range of mental health problems. CBT is based on the idea that how we think (cognition), how we feel (emotion), and how we act (behavior) all interact together. Our thoughts

determine our feelings, and our behavior. Therefore, negative and unrealistic thoughts cause us distress and result in problems.

When a person suffers from psychological distress, the ways in which they interpret situations become skewed, which in turn has a negative impact on the actions they take. CBT aims to help people become aware of making negative interpretations, and of behavioral patterns which reinforce distorted thinking. Cognitive therapy helps people develop alternative ways of thinking and behavior, to reduce their psychological distress. It is an umbrella term for many different therapies that share some common elements. There are two forms of CBT: Rational Emotive Behavioral Therapy (REBT) developed by Albert Ellis in the 1950s, and Cognitive Therapy, developed by Aaron T. Beck in 1960. Both of them foster the same belief, that thoughts produce feelings, and feelings produce behavior.

The general assumptions of CBT are: A) Abnormality of thinking stems from faulty thinking or cognitive deficiencies, lack of planning, or cognitive distortion; B) This cognition causes distortion in the way we see things; C) We interact with the world through our mental representation of it. If our mental representation is inaccurate, or ways of reasoning are inadequate, then our emotion and behavior may become distorted.

Cognitive psychology adopts a scientific approach to observable mental processes by advancing precise models and conducting experiments upon behavior to confirm or refuse them. Full understanding, prediction and control in psychology is probably unobtainable due to the huge complexity of environmental, mental and biological influences upon even simple behaviors (i.e. extraneous variables cannot be controlled).

4) Humanism. Pundits of this field believe objective reality is less important than a person's subjective perception and understanding of the world. It is a psychological perspective that emphasizes the study of the whole person, and tends to look at human behavior not only through the eyes of observation, but through the eyes of the person doing the behavior. It also rejects determinism in favor of free will, aiming to arrive at a unique and in-depth understanding. It has no set theories. As Miller (1969) put it, psychology is a means of promoting human welfare.

5) Narrative Therapy is a technique in which the patient is engaged completely, by writing his own narrative; either the story of his life, or his present condition. Following that, the patient may write an alternative for his life, an ideal situation in dealing with his difficulty. The patient is keenly aware of his condition since it has been put in writing, and he becomes an active participant in finding a solution to his difficulty. I have found this technique effective with patients who have some education, and some insights into their life difficulty.

<u>Words Can Change Our Brain</u>. Sticks and stones may break your bones, but words can change your brain. That is right, according to Dr. Andrew Newberg and Mark Robert. Words can literally change your brain. A single word has the power to influence the expression of genes that regulate physical and emotional stress. Positive words, such as peace and love, can alter the expression of genes, strengthen our frontal lobes and promote the brain's cognitive functioning. They propel the motivational center of the brain into action, and build resiliency.

Conversely, hostile language can disrupt specific genes that play a key part in the production of neurochemicals that protect us from stress. Humans are hardwired to worry-the brain protects us from threats to our survival —so our thoughts naturally go there first. However, a single negative word can increase the activity in our amygdala, the fear center of the brain. This releases dozens of stress-producing hormones and neurotransmitters, which in turn interrupt our brain's functioning, especially regarding logic, reason, and language. Anger words send alarm messages through the brain, and they partially shut down the logic and reasoning center located in the frontal lobes. Thus, using the right words can transform our reality.

By holding positive and optimistic words in your mind, you stimulate frontal lobe activity. This area includes the specific language center that connects directly to the motor cortex responsible for moving you into action. And as research has shown, the longer you concentrate on positive words, the more you begin to affect other areas of the brain. Functions in the parietal lobe start to change, which changes your perception of yourself and the people you interact with. A positive view of yourself will bias you toward seeing the good in others, whereas a negative self-image will move you toward being suspicious and doubtful of others. Over time, the structure of your thalamus will also change in response to your conscious words, thoughts, and feelings, and we believe that the thalamus change affects the way in which you perceive reality.

There is the old question: how many psychologists does it take to change a light bulb? Only one psychologist, but the bulb must really <u>want</u> to be changed. This joke reflects a fundamental point about psychology. Any change that happens in your life must come from you and your own efforts. Although a psychologist can guide you, no one can do the work for you. Psychology is not about getting rid of symptoms, unlike politics and even unlike medicine. Psychology is not about waging war or getting control of anything. Instead, it is about making peace within, by listening to and understanding your symptoms. And curiously enough, once you listen to, rather than fear, your symptoms, you can be enlightened by a profound wisdom that will become a great blessing to your life. However, insight in itself is not sufficient to bring about behavioral change. For psychological change to occur, a person must react to insight with a shock, and a strong desire to change and no longer blame others for his own misery. He will see the ugliness of his own behavior for what it is, and be motivated to change the present. It can be said the only basis for lasting psychological change is the insight and the desire to change.

There is a study by Brent Robert, professor of psychology at the University of Illinois at Champaign-Urbana, whereby he and his colleagues reviewed 144 studies involving more than 15,000 people. The studies all employed some type of intervention, such as talk therapy, anti-depressant medications, meditation, cognitive training, and an assessment of personality traits. But none intentionally tried to change personality. There was a significant change in the personalities of people not in the control group in the studies, the researchers found. The biggest change was seen in people with psychological disorders, such as depression and anxiety, but even healthy people had some personality change.

The personality trait that changed the most was neuroticism, a tendency to experience negative emotions such as depression, anxiety, and extroversion, into a tendency to be sociable, outgoing, and experience more positive emotions. People always think that it is a lot of easier to change their partner's personality than they can change their own.

Group therapy changes our thoughts, attitudes, self-concepts, motivation, values and expectations. We focus on the following for changes, by using a variety of psychological tools:

1) Changing your self-concept and building self-esteem; 2) Increase self-awareness by self-confirmation and feedback; 3) Challenge irrational ideas through rational-emotive therapy; 4) Determinism, accepting all behavior as lawful; 5) Trying new life-styles (fixed role therapy); 6) Paradoxical intentions -- doing the unwanted to get rid of it; 7) Increasing motivation; 8) Straight thinking -- common sense; 9) Developing attitudes that help; 10) Learning new behaviors; 11) Unlearning old behaviors; 12) Extension; 13) Self-monitoring; 14) Biofeedback; 15) Exposure therapy.

Also, 16) Response prevention; 17) Flooding and rational override; 18) Relapse prevention; 19) Rear motivation; 20) Aversion therapy; 21) Cognitive restructuring; 22) Changing thoughts and beliefs; 23) Group therapy and AA; 24) Hypnosis; 25) Present moment thinking. Acceptance in this method of treatment, is accepting reality, and committing to change. Acceptance refers to seeing things as they are, and not as you think they should be. In Dialectical Behavioral Therapy, Marsha Linehan speaks of radical acceptance; recognizing reality, then identifying the place from which you must start in order to change.

Chapter Twenty Two

The Peaceful Mind and Creative Thoughts

As a rule, what is out of sight disturbs the mind more seriously than what we see. Creative individuals have fresh perceptions and may make important discoveries that only they know about.

How do we define peace of mind? The word peace has its root in Sanskrit, which is *Shanti*. Peace of mind is a state of mental and emotional calmness, with no worries, fears or stress. In this state, the mind is quiet, and you experience a sense of happiness and freedom.

Does peace of mind exist? How can we attain a peaceful mind? The mind is never peaceful; no mind is in peace. The very nature of the mind is to be tense, to be in conflict, and to be confused. The mind can never be clear; it cannot have clarity, because of the confusion and cloudiness that dominates our thoughts. Clarity is possible without the mind, peace is possible without the mind, silence is possible without the mind. Thus, when we try to attain silence of the mind, we are moving to a realm of impossible dimension (OSHO).

Peace of mind is intrinsically impossible. Peace happens only when the mind is not involved. It is not peace of mind, it is peace beyond the mind, but how can you manage it? It is almost like a lotus flower; it grows in mud and water. It is a miracle of nature that out of dirty mud and water, comes one of the most beautiful flowers in existence. But mud and water is not the lotus flower. The lotus flower blossoms only when the lotus plant has gone beyond the mud, and beyond the water. It has transcended both, and opens up to the sun and sky, and releases its fragrance on the wind. Although it comes from mud, it is not mud anymore; it transcended.

How do we transcend, or how do we attain transcendence? Remember that whatever is happening around you is rooted in the mind. Your mind is always the cause; it is the projector, and outside there are only screens. You project yourself. If you feel the projection is ugly, then change the mind. If whatever comes from the mind is hellish and nightmarish, then drop the mind. Work with the mind, do not work with the screen, do not just paint it, <u>change</u> it.

The serious problem here is you think you are the mind. So how can you drop it? You can drop everything, change everything, repaint, redecorate, rearrange, but you are not the mind. Meditation may show you are not the mind. If even for a few moments the mind stops, you are still there. On the contrary, you are more, overflowing with being. When the mind stops it is as if a drainage which was continuously draining you has stopped. Suddenly, you are overflowing with energy, vitality and you feel more into life.

Step out from the mind; the watcher is never part of the mind. The mind is just like a movie screen on which thoughts, dreams, imagination, projections, desires and a thousand and one things pass continually. The watcher is not the screen; he is sitting in the movie hall. The problem arises when the watcher becomes identified with something on the movie screen. If your identification with thoughts is creating confusion, it brings you down into the mind; the watcher is usually far above it. To get centered in your watching is the only way to achieve peace.

The fact is, you have gathered a lot of rubbish over the years, and this rubbish will come out. The mind has never been given the freedom to throw away this rubbish. When given a chance, the mind will run like a wild horse that has broken his reins. Let it run you, just sit and watch. To watch, just watch, is the art of patience. You will want to ride the horse, to direct it this way or that, because that is your old habit. You will have to exercise patience in order to break this habit.

Wherever the mind goes, merely watch, do not try to enforce any order, because all things are connected. Speak your mind. Try to speak thoughts out loud so that you can also hear them, because within the mind the thoughts are subtle and there is the fear you may not be very conscious of them, and separate yourself from your thought, but you have to be absolutely unbiased and neutral.

You have to empty your mind patiently every six months, because all your life you have done nothing but load it with thoughts. If you persist patiently and diligently, then every six months is enough. Then you can hear the footsteps of silence, and experience the art of listening.

Recently our knowledge and control of the external world have increased considerably; we have extraordinary material development. But human happiness has not increased, and suffering around the world has not decreased. On the contrary, it could be said there are greater problems and more unhappiness than ever before. Therefore, happiness and suffering co-exist within the mind; their origins are not to be found outside the mind, if we want to find lasting happiness.

If we study the different types of the mind, how they are generated, and what effect they have on our lives, it is difficult to distinguish the virtuous mind from the non-virtuous mind, and we are clueless about how to cultivate the former and abandon the latter. Why is it necessary to understand the mind? Because, happiness and suffering are states of mind, so if we want to be free from suffering and enjoy true happiness we need to possess a thorough understanding of the mind and how to control it. There is no other way to definitely improve the quality of life, both now and in the future.

To bring more peace of mind to life, there are a few things that we have to apply, so we can have a peace of mind:

1) Minimize the time you spend reading newspapers, or watching the news on TV. Since most of the news is negative, and we cannot do anything about it, it just makes us anxious and stressed.

2) Stay away from negative conversation and negative people, because their words and thoughts sink into your unconscious and effect your state of mind.

3) Do not hold grudges; learn to forgive and forget. Nurturing ill feelings and grievances hurts you.

4) Do not be jealous of others. Jealousy means you have low self-esteem, and consider yourself inferior to others, which leads to lack of peace of mind.

5) Accept what cannot be changed. We face numerous inconveniences in life, and we have to put up with them.

6) Do not dwell on the past. The past is not here anymore, so why think about it? Do not evoke unpleasant memories.

7) Learn to be patient and tolerant with others.

8) Do not take everything too personally. A certain degree of emotional and mental detachment is very helpful.

9) Learn to focus your mind. When you can focus, you can more easily reject worries and anxieties.

10) Meditation is not everyone's cup of tea, but if you have the time, try it, and you will become more peaceful, relaxed and happy. Once you have inner peace, that will lead to external peace. There is a raging war in our heart and mind. This inner war clouds our thoughts, consumes our energies and makes us stupid.

Chapter Twenty Three

How to Acquire A Super Mind

A person can train his mind the way gymnasts train their muscles. -- Socrates

When you have discipline over your mind, you will be able to reprogram your thoughts, even though many of the functions of the mind are outside of conscious control. Whether we maintain true control over any mental function is the central debate about free will. This lack of autonomy is the foundation for almost all the mind's labors, laid long before our ancestors evolved consciousness (Archetypes). Understanding our mind and consciousness are the most fascinating topics of the day. The study of the mind is a rapidly evolving field and captivating discovery.

You are not your thoughts; thoughts comes and go of their own accord. Water takes the shape of whatever container holds it, whether it be in a glass, a vase or a riverbank. Likewise, your mind will create and manifest according to the images you habitually think about in your daily thinking. This is how our destiny is created. A new life is created by new thoughts.

Deepak Chopra said, "we do not just have experiences, we metabolize them." Every experience turns into a coded chemical signal that will alter the life of your cells, either small or big, for a minute or for a lifetime.

The power of omniscience, telepathy, clairvoyance, and mind reading, can remove the memories of the past, and make the mind powerful enough to clear all impressions and liberate us, because thought is non-material in nature. However, the result of thoughts produced by the physical brain have to be physical in nature and are governed by physical laws.

Thoughts develop in the brain when neurons fire in a certain portion of the brain. The neurons communicate with each other via feedback loops

146

(through chemical signals) and even photonically (via light) and through synchronization. As one thought emerges and subsides (if not enough energy is provided to it), it is replaced by another thought, emerging from another part of the brain, and in this way brain chatter takes place. The thought structure is like a hologram, and could be the reason why most of our thinking is geometric in nature, and we seem to visualize everything in terms of shapes and geometry. A billion neurons fire in laser like fashion for a long time on a single thought.

Once the mind cultivates the habit of focusing on a particular thought for a long time, the neural pathways for other thoughts sublimate and regroup to provide energy for this single thought. Then a new neural pathway is established, which can dissolve the old memory, because the human brain is pliable and capable of creating new neural pathways and connections; this is neuroplasticity.

Michael Hogan and Steve Jobs advised students not to let the noise of other's opinions drown out their own inner voice, but rather have the courage to follow their hearts and intuition. Psychology seeks to understand how intuition works, and may deceive us. We must learn to master our subtle, intuitive mind, and cultivate greater strength, joy, creative and reflective capacities.

Intuition is often assumed to be faster and easier than rational deliberation. According to Carol Rogers, to become a fully functioning person requires developing the ability to trust your instincts and cultivate intuition, as well as spontaneous modes of self-expression. Carl Jung characterized optimal mental health as including the ability to maintain openness to messages from a deeper level of the unconscious.

The Invisible Gorilla, a book by Chabris and Simon (2010) revealed that we have reservoirs of untapped mental ability, just waiting to be effortlessly accessed. Unfortunately, current society reinforces laziness, and our tendency to select quick and easy fixes which do not allow us to find the real capacity of our mind. We need to understand how the mind works, and why people act the way they do. Often, it's not because of stupidity, arrogance, or lack of focus, but because of everyday illusions that affect us all. Socrates said, "know thyself", and that is the hard part of modern psychology, because we have distorted views of our reality.

Recent scientific evidence suggests that the brain is full of sexual chemicals, and their increased concentration in it helps in memory enhancement. As memory increases so does the ability of concentration. Thus, the desire to save these chemicals could be the basis of celibacy.

You have billions upon billions of neurons. In fact, if your brain neurons were laid out end to end, they would stretch all the way to the moon and back. But the secret to a lively brain is not your number of neurons, but the diversity of interconnections between those neurons. Researchers like Dr. Marion Diamond, who analyzed Albert Einstein's brain, found it was different in only one way. Einstein had more interconnections between his neurons. Such supply of interconnections is not inherited. No one is born with such a brain, it is created. Your brain follows the same rules as your muscles: use it or lose it.

Unused neuronal interconnections actually shrink and die, but if you engage in regular mental workouts these interconnections then expand and strengthen. If you manage to overload your brain with the right kind of sensory information, the brain is forced physically to reorganize itself and grow. This will expand mind power into entirely new dimensions of thought, and you will experience an actual super state of being.

The brilliant American psychologist William James said, "compared to what we should be, we are only half alive. We are making use of only a small part of our mind power. Deep down inside of us are vast powers we know nothing of, and are never used." We are all blessed with awesome potential super mind power, and this power can answer and solve any of our problems, dilemmas, and personal challenges. You have the power to create a perfect life. If you learn how to unleash the vast unlimited potential of your mind power, infinite resources are at your command. You are not limited in any way by your environment, your background, your intelligence or even by lack of money.

There are three things that tap into the power of your mind: 1) Beliefs; whatever belief that you have either empowering or disempowering, lifts you up, or pulls you down. 2) Focus on what you want and do not focus on what you do not want. Try to concentrate, or be mindful, and you will see the value of it. 3) Meditate. The Iced Man was a dedicated meditator; he focused on healing his dead frozen toes and healed them.

Then, to acquire a super brain, you need to tap into such energy. The majority of people do not even bother to think about it, let alone unearth it.

Thus, we live our life half dizzy, with the unconscious mind in the driver's seat. This is why we have high rates of depression and anxiety, because we keep playing the same scenario over and over and create a synaptic connection in our brain.

Chapter Twenty Four

How to Master Your Mind

The wisdom of poetry:

Why do you cling to the arrows shot at you?
Insults, wounds....
Time heals you see
Why hold so tightly
Do these things to set you free;
Why inject yourself with these poisons of the mind:
Anxiety, greed, anger and despair.

There is only one corner of the universe you can be certain of improving, and this is your self (Aldous Huxley). What do we mean by self? It is our personality, and it can be shaped by the way we perceive ourselves privately. Our perception comes through our experiences, whether positive or negative. Thus, we have to be extremely careful to have positive experiences. Surround yourself with positive people who try to bring the best out in you, not the people who are critical or negative towards you.

Today, the concept we have to pay attention to, and integrate in the fabric of our thinking is "Try to use your mind, do not let your mind use you." The best example of the brain using you is when it imposes a false reality on you. All phobias are distortions of reality. Bear in mind, the stakes are very high when it comes to letting your brain use you. But if you start to use it instead, the rewards are unlimited.

Repetition glues old habits into the brain. Nursing a negative emotion is the surest way to block positive emotion. Nothing solidifies a memory like emotion. How to transform negative emotions to positive ones is the real challenge facing us.

If you want to know what your thoughts were like in the past, look at your body today. If you want to know what your body will be like in the future, look at your thoughts today.

We may suffer not from disease of the body, but from delusion of the mind. As Julius Caesar said, as a rule, what is out of sight disturbs men's minds more seriously than what they see. There are three poisons that take all the joy from our lives: anger, attachment, and ignorance. If we take real control over these poisonous thoughts, then we really are mastering our mind.

To master your mind, you have to detoxify it from overthinking, through the following steps:

1) Stop consuming the news. All of news is bad, and we cannot do anything about it. It is just war, peace, conflicts, ignorance, bad health, greed, abuse, social injustice, manipulation and savagery. Why bother to watch? You do not miss anything. Several studies show people who do not watch the news tend to have a less negative view of the world and less illness (like high blood pressure).

2) Soak the mind with positive juice, Our mind is a sponge, it absorbs almost everything it encounters, from the negative comment a work colleague made a year ago, to some awful things we conjure up in a dream. Unfortunately, we cannot help internalizing all the things our senses pick up. All the worries of the world get into our head and do not seem to leave, causing us to overthink our lives and the actions we want to take.

3) Get up and get to work on a goal, a project, or task. Once you have such goals, you have the blueprint for your life, and that should motivate you to be more involved in your personal life rather than living aimlessly.

4) Another component of mastering your mind is to cultivate positive virtuous thoughts of mercy, love, purity, forgiveness, integrity, generosity, and humility, in the garden of your mind. Then the negative vicious thoughts of hatred, lust, anger, greed, and pride will die by themselves.

5) Do things which the mind does not want you to do, and do not do a thing the mind wants you to do. In other words, challenge yourself greatly and sincerely.

We may detox our body, because we want to look good and feel good. But most importantly, detox the mind from overthinking, because we have a career to grow, and a life to live.

Manage good thinking without undue anxiety. Differentiate thinking from obsessive thinking. Thinking includes reasoning, reflecting, pondering, judging, analyzing and evaluating an idea or decision. It is using your mind in a creative, effective manner. Thinking tends to be product goal-oriented, and action-oriented. Obsession, in contrast, is having your mind excessively focused on a single emotion or event. It hinders your ability to relax, is counterproductive, and can be crippling to you.

The mind is a mischievous imp; it is like a jumping monkey. It must be disciplined daily, then it might gradually come under control. It is only by the practical training of your mind that you can prevent bad thoughts and actions from arising. Watch your mind very carefully, be vigilant, and be on the alert. Do not allow waves of irritability, jealousy, anger, hatred, envy, anxiety and lust to arise from the mind. These dark waves are enemies of peace, wisdom, and tranquility. Just as you check the intruder or enemy at the gate of your house, you need to check the disturbing thought before it strikes deep inside your psyche. Nip it in the bud; do not allow the thought to even rise in your mind.

The mind is like a wheel which revolves endlessly with tremendous velocity; it generates new thoughts with every revolution. The fewer the desires, the fewer the thoughts. The fewer the thoughts, the greater inner peace and inner strength, which achieve by reduction of thoughts. As a loose tooth needs to be pulled, your unwanted thoughts need to be rooted out. Thoughts pop into our mind without our permission faster than mosquito bites on a sweltering summer afternoon.

Descartes, the father of modern philosophy, pointed out the biggest curse of human beings when he said "I Think, therefore I am." That you and I can think, reflect on the past, imagine the future, even to be conscious of our own consciousness, is what distinguishes humans from all others animals.

Overall, we cannot control our mind, but we can regulate our pattern of thoughts by the following:

1) Instantly replace unwanted thoughts. Instantly neutralize the power of a negative thought; calmly and deliberately replace it with its opposite, a positive equivalent thought. For instance, if you think to yourself, "I am not good enough for women, I may never succeed with them," Replace that thought with "I am good enough and success comes to me easily." You can also use "cancel, cancel." Each time you catch yourself thinking an unwanted thought, tell yourself and the universe "cancel," and immediately follow it up with a positive statement. Change the way you look at things and the things you look at change.

2) Tame your dominant thoughts and your random thoughts will follow suit. It is estimated that the average person has between 2,000 and 7,000 thoughts a day. This is evidence enough to suggest that your goal should not be to control every thought. It is your dominant thoughts that you need to bring under your conscious control, because these thoughts largely determine your mental attitudes.

   Buddha said, "all that we are is the result of what we have thought; the mind is everything what we think we become." In a nutshell, your life is the perfect mirror of your thoughts and beliefs.

3) Rise above your emotion. Be the witness, not the puppet, so that you can learn to transcend the law of polarity and rise above your emotion. By doing so, you become the witness rather than a puppet being flung around by the swing of your thoughts.

Some techniques to master unwanted thoughts:

1) Forget suppression. If you try to suppress your negative thoughts, they will become like a coiled spring; the more you suppress the coiled springs, the more pressure is built upon it. If you let go of your hand even slightly, the coiled springs jumps much more vigorously. If you suppress]negative thoughts, the will come out violently, and the situation will go from bad to worse.

2) Resist the outburst technique. If you let out your thoughts and express your anger, for example, you may temporarily feel relaxed, but later on you feel guilty and worse. That exercise makes you more negative and angry; it is a vicious cycle and eventually may lead to mental imbalances, which are the source of all our disturbances.

3) Still the mind technique. This is very a difficult one unless you are a yogi or a sage man who has been doing it and training their mind for a long time.

4) Substitution technique. Since all these techniques are not effective, basically, you cannot control the mind, and it is very incorrect to say that you control your mind, because the mind cannot be controlled. What you <u>can</u> do is regulate the mind. Thus, here are a few examples in how to regulate the mind. If you enter a dark room, you cannot see anything. But if you switch on the light, the entire room is filled with light. The darkness vanished automatically. You did not attempt to drive away nor suppress the darkness; You only turned on the light switch. You enabled the light to come in, which drove away the darkness automatically. Similarly in the case of your mind, bring positive thoughts to it, which will automatically drive away your negative thoughts. The mind cannot be empty by any means, thus you have to bring in some thoughts

Some steps for substitution techniques to regulate your mind:

1) The most crucial one is to replace negative thoughts with positive ones. Bring positive thoughts to your mind without fighting the negative ones; gradually they will seep into your conscious mind. Let's say you have one liter of filthy water and you need to replace it with clean drinking water, (metaphorically speaking, which is like the mind). But there is a condition: you cannot pour out the filthy water and put in clean water. The alternative way is to go to the water stream where the clean water is flowing, and immerse the filthy bottle in the stream (the stream of your positive thoughts). You will find after few minutes, the entire bottle is filled with clean water.

In summary, try to flood your brain with positive, encouraging, meaningful messages to replace the negative ones. You cannot empty your mind of negative thoughts, but force upon your mind some positive appealing thoughts, and that will keep your mind busy and will push out negative messages.

2) Be mindful of every single action you do in your daily life, even silly things like putting your car keys on the table, or brushing your teeth.

You are holding the leash of your mind by focusing on what you do at hand.

3) Try to train your eyes to see pleasant and beautiful sights, because the mind is like a computer; whatever you put in it will come back to you. We have five sensory organs (eyes, ears, nose, mouth and hands); all providing input to the mind. Seeing beautiful sights will bring positive input to your mind.

4) Prayers and meditation can be very powerful tools to tame and cultivate the mind.

5) Hear pleasing things like music, and avoid hearing filthy words, or violent arguments.

6) Speak softly and positively, and avoid harsh words or criticism, which we all are so good at.

7) Eat live food and avoid dead food. We have two kinds of food, either life-draining energy food, or life-giving energy food, which can be very essential to nourish the brain.

8) Smell good fragrances do not mask you natural body fragrance.

9) Involve yourself in doing good deeds for other people. Get out of yourself so you can find yourself.

10) Go to a spiritual place and give yourself the gift of nature as often as you can, and seek some solitude once in a while.

11) When negative thoughts enter your mind, do not fight them; rather just let the pass. Do not have interest in them, or you may try to examine them. As is said, do not invite them in and serve them tea.

12) Have a daily subliminal positive mantra to live by, like my life is really beautiful, I am a fortunate person, and there are a lot of wonderful things in my life.

13) Be around people who tend to bring the best out in you, and by any means avoid the people who tap into your dark side.

14) Liberate yourself internally by cooling the fire of anger and discontent.

15) When negative thoughts arise, and you choose to water them with the power of attention, they will grow, so starve them. Do not pay attention to them and let them pass.

16) Leave your front door and your back door open. Let thoughts come and go, and do not ever try to investigate them. Let them pass without noticing them.

17) Use humor in your daily life to overcome many things, and never take yourself too seriously in life, because no one gets out of it alive.

18) Never argue with your mind. It is like challenging your thought with another thought, which will not work; it will produce the opposite result. A knife cannot cut itself.

19) If someone is throwing garbage into your house, you will fight with that person. But if someone is throwing garbage into your mind, do not fight with that person. Instead, ignore the garbage.

20) Finally, have belief in the spiritual part of life. There is a great master (God) of this universe; let this power reside deep down in your heart. You are part of a grand plan that already has been designed for you. Take the ride in the boat of life without resistance.

What is a paradigm shift? Paradigm comes from Greek *paradeigmia*, which means pattern or example, thought pattern, or sub-conscious conditioning. Shift means a radical change in somebody's basic assumption about their approach to something. We look here to our higher mental faculties:

1) Reason; 2) Memory; 3) Perception; 4) Will; 5) Intuition; 6) Imagination.

Since inception we are programmed genetically. When we come into the world, we receive more programming through our environment. Both of these programs play a major role in life, and we spend most of our life trying to free ourselves from them. The first programming happens while in the womb, and it depends on what kind of food our mother ate, and what kind of psychological condition that she was in. Both factors can shape our life later on, and have serious consequences for us.

The second programming occurs when we are just young children, called a paradigm. It helps us form many habits, a collection of fixed ideas in our unconscious mind. All these habits constitute our paradigm. Anything we receive from our surroundings tends to get into our neurons and become part of our frame of mind.

Our behavior is then directed and managed by this paradigm, a collection of all habits, attitudes, perceptions and patterns of thinking. If you want to make a change in your life, the paradigm tends to resist the change, because the materials in the unconscious mind do not correspond with the reality. It has rooted in the synapses of our brain; this why we cannot make change. We have to replace one thought with another thought, or bring another positive thought to take over. If we want to regulate our mind, we need to free ourselves from the early paradigm that has been established through our early programming. This book has a plethora of techniques for you to use, and to make your life an enjoyable journey.

Chapter Twenty Five

Brain Food

There are few things you can do to improve the overall quality of your life better than feeding your brain the right food. Undoubtedly, it will keep you happy, physically healthy, mentally clear, motivated, and ready to handle the stress of life that is thrown at all of us. This is why the old saying says "we are what we eat." It is absolutely true, because our brain is a hungry little organ weighing only 3 pounds, but, it uses 20% of our daily caloric intake. Give your brain the physical nutrients it needs. What you feed yourself, you also feed your brain. You cannot expect optimal mental function on a fast food diet. You also need good supply of clean water, so you cannot be dehydrated.

The brain needs a lot of nutrition to keep it humming along smoothly, but not the kind you can get from a bottle, or cans, or frozen pizza. Try to get your nutrition for your brain from whole foods. Provide it with carbohydrates for energy, proteins to create brain chemicals and fats to build healthy brain cells.

Sadly, most people eat for taste, or convenience, or for the waistline. But you have to think that eating for your brain is a lot smarter. The quality of eating is neglected by most people; they tend to eat what is available in their refrigerator. Often, they even do not think about what they put in their mouth. A number of illnesses have increased dramatically over the last 50 years, such as diabetes, high blood pressure, high cholesterol, heart disease, and breathing problems, all as a result of not taking care, or paying serious attention to what we put in our mouths.

We have to eat to have a sharper and healthier mind, but does our diet make us smarter? Without a shred of doubt, yes it does, and this book will review all the important foods you need to consume, so you can be a healthy and smart person. Eating well is good for your mental as well as your physical health. The brain requires nutrients just like your heart, lungs or muscles. But which foods are particularly important to keep our grey matter happy? There are many foods you have to focus on to nurture your brain:

1) Whole grains. The brain cannot work without energy, and whole grains offer a steady supply of glucose with a low glycemic index, which releases slowly into the bloodstream, keeping you mentally alert throughout the day. Focus on brown cereal, wheat bran and barley bread.

2) Oily fish. Essential fatty acids cannot be made by the body; they have to be obtained through diet. The most effective one is Omega-3 fats with EPA and DHA, which occur naturally in oily fish, such as salmon, trout, mackerel, herring, sardines and kippers. If you do not have DHA you are at higher risk of developing a loss of memory, as well as Alzheimer's Disease. There are other sources of these essential fatty acids. You may find them in flaxseed oil, soybean oil, pumpkin seeds and walnut oil. So try to include those types of food in your daily intake, and do not be lazy. Undoubtedly, you will be amazed by feeling so well, and the abundance of energy you will have.

3) Blueberries. Tufts University research showed that consuming some berries daily may be effective in improving or delaying short term memory loss. They are available everywhere, so you have no excuse whatsoever. Just go and buy them!

4) Tomatoes have lycopene, an antioxidant that works against free radicals, which can damage the cells, and eventually cause you to develop dementia.

5) Vitamins B6, B12, and folic acid, are vital and known to reduce the level of homocysteine in the blood; if the level is elevated it may increase the risk of stroke, or cognitive impairment.

6) Blackcurrants. Vitamin C has the power to increase mental agility. The best source is the blackcurrant.

7) Pumpkin seeds. A handful of pumpkin seeds a day, is all you need to get your supply of zinc which enhances thinking skills. Also, a handful of pumpkin seeds a day, keeps the urologist away.

8) Broccoli is a great source of vitamin K, which we need to improve brain power.

9) Sage has a great reputation to improve memory. No doubt, it is worth adding to your plate.

10) Walnuts have Vitamin E, which might help prevent cognitive decline. All nuts are great sources of vitamins, along with leafy green vegetables like asparagus, olives, eggs, brown rice and whole grains. There are other essential foods also for our brain, such as hazelnuts, Brazil nuts, almonds, cashews, peanuts, sunflower seeds, sesame seeds, and Tahini, which is a food from the east.

11) Coffee and Green Tea are good for your brain.

12) Turmeric. Just put it with warm water and drink. It is also an antioxidant.

13) Onions. Make them a staple of your diet, and you will see amazing health.

14) Apples, grapes and the almighty fig.

15) Olive oil improves your skin, prevents constipation, and enhances the smell of food.

16) Eggs, which must be naturally fed, but not much from the yolk (the yellow part).

17) Coconut oil. There is a lot of talk about the nutritional value of it.

18) Avocado is called the supreme food for our body. These buttery fruits are rich in monounsaturated fat, which contribute to healthy blood flow in the brain.

19) All kind of root vegetables, such as potatoes, carrots, and beets.

20) Rosemary stimulates nerve growth and reverses cell damage.

21) Finally, the food we all love -- dark chocolate! You have to buy 70% or higher dark chocolate. It is a brain food that contains a pleasure-giving substance called endorphins; it has contains flavonoids, caffeine and the bromine, which all are important for memory and focus, as well as attention.

There are certain foods we need to include in our daily intake, such as green tea. It is an antioxidant that helps stop beta-amyloid proteins from harming brain cells or blocking proteins that build the brain, and it destroys plaques. Another food that is powerful is kale and other cruciferous vegetables. These "super foods" contain powerful antioxidants that can protect your brain from toxic free radicals.

<u>Balanced blood sugar</u>. Sugar is your brain's super fuel, but too much sugar in the blood creates hyperactivity, especially in children. Excess sugar in the blood gets dumped into storage as abdominal fat. The rate in which sugar enters brain cells and other cells of the body is called the glycemic index (GI) of a particular food. Food with a high glycemic index stimulates the pancreas to secrete a lot of insulin, which causes the sugar to quickly empty from the blood into the cells, producing the ups and downs of blood sugar and the roller coaster behavior that goes with them. Food with a low GI does not push the pancreas to secrete so much insulin, so the blood sugar tends to be steadier.

Good brain food with low GI includes: grapefruit, apples, cherries, oranges, and grapes all have low GI. Fruit juice is not good, because the fiber of the fruit slows down the absorption of sugar. A whole apple will be more brain-friendly than apple juice. Cereal and grains, like oatmeal and bran have the lowest GI over other foods with favorable GI. Vegetables and legumes such as kidney beans, chick peas, and lentils, all have low GI.

Dairy products, like milk and yogurt have a low GI. Even though milk has a bad reputation, it is still considered a good food.

Humans imitate animals in most instances; grazing is the cow's way of eating just little by little, all day long. That style of eating is more beneficial to humans too, because the body takes a little food then digests it, and later takes another portion of food, rather than gorging itself with a lot of food in one meal or late at night.

Food can be a sedative due to neurotransmitters. Two amino acids influence the four top neurotransmitters, which are: serotonin, which is made from the amino acid tryptophan, and dopamine, epinephrine, norepinephrine, which are made from the amino acid tyrosine. Serotonin is the neurotransmitter that relaxes the brain.

Having a nourishing, well rounded diet can give your brain the best chance of avoiding disease. If your diet is unbalanced, you need to investigate what is the best for you, and try not to give in to the temptations of junk food.

<u>Feeding the brain of the baby</u>. The most rapid brain growth occurs during the first year of life, with the infant brain tripling in size by the first birthday. During this stage of rapid central nervous system growth, the brain uses 60 percent of the total energy consumed by the infant, and the brain itself is 60 percent fat. Fats are major components of the brain cell membrane and the

myelin sheath around each nerve. So, it makes sense that getting enough fat and the right kinds of fat can greatly affect brain development and performance. In fact, during the first year, around 50% of an infant's daily calories come from fat. Mother Nature knows how important fat is for a baby, thus, 50% of mother's milk is fat. Try to breast feed the baby by any means.

Finally, there is no denying that as we age chronologically, our body ages right along with us. But research is showing that you can increase your chance of maintaining a healthy brain well into old age, if you add these smart foods to your daily eating regimen. In conclusion food is the utmost important factor to a healthy brain and healthy memory, as well as preventing us from developing early Alzheimer's Disease. Most scientific research shows that lack of proper nutrients for the brain can have dire consequences for our cognitive functioning.

Conclusions

The basic concept of this book is there is no scientific study more vital to man than the study of his own mind. The mind is its own place, and in itself can make a heaven of hell, or hell of heaven (James Allen). This book is a comprehensive attempt to explore most of the facets of the human brain. When we define mind, the mind is a brain in action. The brain is the biological structure of our mind's faculties, which are perception, imagination, and thinking.

Why is it necessary to understand our mind? The answer is simple and logical. Happiness and suffering are states of mind, so if we want to be free from suffering and enjoy true happiness, we need to possess a thorough understanding of the mind and how to control it. There is no other way we can definitely improve our quality of life, both now and in the future.

In early life, we establish the paradigm of our thoughts, from birth to age six. The brain waves of the child are delta and theta; both of these brain waves are like a hypnotic stage, whereby the child absorbs the outside world without any questioning, just like a sponge, and does not differentiate between reality and imagination, and is not critical of any thing around him. Thus, the materials absorbed in the early life are stored in the unconscious mind, and tend to have a serious influence over life later on.

Moreover, the constitution of our personality has also been established by the time we reach age six. We may have a hard time in the later stages of our lives to untangle what has been woven in the fabric of our mind in these early stages. Thus, childhood can be very crucial for our brain development and function.

For the last 50 years we have built the best roads, the best hospitals, the best airplanes to fly, and wealth has increased, almost all over the world. But our level of happiness has decreased, because happiness depends on our thoughts, not on outside materialistic advancement. We have to focus on our thinking and how we change our frame of our mind, from being nervous, anxious, depressed, to being a serene, joyful, and happy individual.

If we examine the nature of thoughts, we see the mind is a mischievous imp. Therefore our mind must be disciplined daily. Otherwise we will become like the child riding an elephant. We are the child and the elephant is our mind, which means our mind is controlling us, and we are not in control of our mind. Our mind is scaring us most of the time, for no obvious logical reason. It tends to exaggerate and fabricate any simple shred of difficulty. And often, it skews our reality, and projects the stored materials of the unconscious mind on reality. We are unhappy people, because we believe our mind.

Bringing our mind under our control can be the most challenging task any individual may ever face. Philosophers and scholars from all walks of life and through many centuries have been wrestling with controlling our stream of thoughts that never stop, to give us relief from the nagging child of the mind.

We should never lose hope regarding how to control the mind. But, let us be clear, there is no such thing as truly controlling the mind. There is regulating the mind, but the mind cannot be controlled by any means. It is always in the command of our personality, and does not stop thinking until we go to the grave.

However, we can use several techniques to regulate our mind, and by practical training we can prevent bad thoughts and actions from arising. We have also to watch our mind very carefully; be vigilant, and be on the alert. Do not allow waves of irritability, jealousy, anger, hatred, envy, anxiety and lust to arise from the mind. These dark waves are the enemies of peace, wisdom and tranquility. Do not allow negative thoughts to even rise in your mind. This book has provided you with practical steps to regulate the mind.

There are myriad disturbing thoughts that occur in our mind, but one of the most torturing is the obsessive thought, which keeps playing in our mind over and over. Often we do not get relief from them until our mental energy has been exhausted. However, you can identify the obsessive thought and try to not give it power, by resisting it. But the nature of the sly mind is if you resist, it will persist. If you ask the mind to go in a certain direction, it will take you in the opposite direction. And that is one of the mysteries of our mind.

We also have observed throughout this book the power of suggestion and how it has a profound impact on people. Any message repeated long enough tends to get into our unconscious mind, and we tend to believe it, without any examination of whether it is real or false.

Sadly enough, politicians are very much aware of this fallibility of human nature. Thus, they fill the TV screen with their unfounded propaganda. Plato said an unexamined life is not worth living. But the sad fact is that most people do not use their mental faculties to examine what has been presented to them. In general, people avoid thinking hard, and are mentally lazy. Or, they may be shallow in the way they approach life and take things wholesale.

The most fascinating part of human brain research in recent history is neuroplasticity. Only a few decades ago, scientists considered the brain to be fixed or hardwired, and considered most forms of brain damage, therefore, to be incurable. Today, we know the brain changes its very structure with each different activity performed. If one part of the brain fails, another part may take over, and this process is called neuroplasticity. The nerve cells in our brains and nervous system are pliable, changeable, malleable and modifiable.

There are many scientific applications for the neuroplasticity of our mind. A good example is work done by Dr. Edward Taub in the United States. He helps paralyzed people re-learn to walk using a technique called Constraint Induced Therapy, which is consistent training to shift function from the dead neurons involved in the paralysis to healthy neurons. This technique has helped many people, even in its brief period of inception. It can be very effective in restoring the health of people, and give hope to those populations.

The other fascinating dynamic of our mind established in recent years is the concept of mirror neurons. Several experiments have been conducted regarding the response of mirror neurons to pain, finding the brain produces a full simulation of observed pain. Although we commonly think of pain as a fundamentally private experience, our brain treats it as an experience shared with others. This neural mechanism is essential for building social ties. It is also very likely these forms of resonance with the painful experiences of others are relatively early mechanisms of empathy, from the evolutionary and developmental point of view.

Thus, mirror neurons make us sympathize with other people who suffer, and immediately we identify with their suffering. Of course, today there are serious scientific applications for this brain phenomenon.

Then we explored the frontier of the unconscious mind, the main theme of this book. The unconscious mind has two primary functions in life; the first is to attract a condition and circumstance according to the predominant thought patterns that reside within it. What you focus on, you attract. With this new information we can begin to understand why your unconscious mind is not limited in any way, and will forever attract to you according to your dominant thoughts. It has no volition of its own, and will simply act upon what resides and vibrates within you.

Moreover, the mind becomes a source of misery, because our unconscious mind or even the conscious mind becomes the garbage bin of society. Society throws trash on you, and you take it, and it becomes part of your psychological makeup. Because, there is no inner engineering that you have done to your unconscious mind; you just let be, and that can have serious consequences on you and on the quality of your life. There is no "inner gardening", whereby you become a good gardener and do your daily job of pulling the weeds from your inner garden. In life, there are a lot difficulties and challenges. Some of those difficulties may leave a very bad residue, and we need serious inner cultivation to get rid of the weeds inside of us, metaphorically speaking.

The unconscious mind is neutral. Thus, if you dwell on past failures, the unconscious mind responds to that. Instead, keep your past and future successes in the front of your mind and get excited about what the future may hold for you. Feel confident, and over time your unconscious mind will dramatically change. The body of research tells us the unconscious mind has difficulty telling the difference between real and vividly imagined, or fake, memory. Therefore, we may use this glitch in the matrix to our best advantage by sheer positive imagination. Consequently, those images become part of our unconscious mind, not just letting the negative events of life dictate our personality.

Our mind works like a nervous dog in the backyard, barking frantically at every passing squirrel, or even smelling a human from a far distance. Even though that human never constitutes any danger to the dog, the dog keeps barking. Over time, dogs that are allowed to continue with such behavior become louder, more frantic, and more aggressive. As annoying and irrational as it may seem to others, the dog's behavior makes sense from the dog's perspective. This is exactly what is happening in our mind. It tends to detect a presumed danger from a very far distance, when in reality there is no danger. We cannot argue with the mind, because it will outmaneuver us by any means. If you ask the mind to think of an object, it seems to obey us for a moment, but soon it will go to its own stored materials, which often are disturbing materials. Because the mind does not obey our command, this book gives you practical steps to regulate the mind and manage disturbing thoughts.

We think that we are our thoughts; this is the common core error in our shared human experience. You are not your thoughts. You are not even the observer of your thoughts. The thoughts that shape your personality came to you from your parents, culture, religion, social system, and so forth. Thus, you have to learn to regulate your mind. Otherwise, it will menace you like the constant dripping of a leaky faucet.

We can spend time each day affirming new programming beliefs, or thoughts. By affirming our new thought patterns, we can effectively change our life and our reality. But, there is another technique which can be extremely effective in living a lifeless disturbed, called mindfulness. You focus on here and now, and try to regulate or manipulate your mind, rather than letting your mind control or manipulate you. If you truly have the leash of your mind in your hands, you suffer less, and ultimately you draw happiness into your life.

References

Anil K Rajvans. (2010). Nature of Human Thought. Nimbkar Agriculture Research Institute [NARI].

Aristotle. (2001). The Basic Works of Aristotle. Modern Library Publisher, Reprinted Edition.

American Psychiatric Association. (2005). Diagnostic and Statistical Manual of Mental Disorders. American Psychological Association Press.

Allen, James. (1901).As A Man Thinketh. De Vorss Publications.

B.F. Skinner. (1965). Science and Human Behavior. Free Press.

Beck, T. Aaron. (1991). Cognitive Therapy and Emotional Disorder. Penguin Publishing.

Begley, Sharon. (2007). Train Your Mind, Change Your Brain. Ballantine Books.

Bjorklund, F. David & Pellegrini, D. Anthony. (2001). The Origins of Human Nature. American Psychological Association Press.

Bucker, Thomas. (2002). Finding the Hope in Lost Kid's Lives. Unlimited Publishing.

Bunge, Mario. (1998). Philosophy of Science: From Problem to Theory. Transactional, Publisher.

Burnham, Terry & Phelan, Jay.(2000). Mean Genes. Perseus Publishing.

Byrne, Rhonda.(2006). The Secret. Beyond World Publication.

Camus, Albert. (1991). The Myth of Sisyphus, and Other Essays. Vintage, Reissue edition Publisher.

Campbell, Joseph. (2011). The Power of Myths. Knopf Doubleday Publisher Group.

Cannon, Walter. (1932). The Wisdom of the Body. Publisher W.W. Norton & Company.

Carlson, E. Linda. (2009). The Art and the Science of Mindfulness. American Psychological Association Press.

Chabris, Christopher & Simon, Daniel. (2010). The Invisible Gorilla, and Other Ways Our Intuitions Deceive Us. Harper Collins, Publisher.

Carlson, Richard. (1999). Don't Sweat the Small Stuff. Simon & Schuster, Publisher.

Chopra, Deepak & Tanzi, Rudolph. (2012). Super Brain. Harmony Books, Publisher.

Chomsky, Noam & Naiman, Arthur. (2011). How the World Works. Soft Skull Press.

C.S. Lewis, (1945). The Great Divorce. Publisher Geoffrey Bles.

Clarke, C, Arthur. (1999). The Final Odyssey. Delrey, Publisher.

Dijksterhuis, Edward. (1986). The Mechanization of the World Picture. Princeton University Press.

Diamond, Marion. (1999). Magic Tree of the Mind. Plum, Publisher.

Doidge, Norman. (2007). The Brain That Changes Itself. Penguin Books.

Dyer, Wayne. (2009). Your Erroneous Zones. Harper Collins Press

Emile, Coue. (2007). Self-Mastery. Arc Manor, Publisher.

Even, Gabrielle. (2011). Hypnotic Healing. Siren-Bookstand.

Einstein, Albert. (1987). The Collection Papers of Albert. Princeton University Press.

Eagleman, David. (1015). The Brain, The Story of You. Canongate Books

Eagleman, David.(2012). The Secret Life of the Brain. Vintage, Publisher.

Eckhart. Tolle. (2000).The Power of Now. New World Library, Publisher.

Ellis, A. (1974). Rational–Emotive Theory. Oxford, Brunner & Mosel, Publisher.

Francis, Raymond. (2007). Never Be Fat Again. Health Communication Corporation.

Francis, Raymond. (2011). Never Fear Cancer Again. Health Communication Corporation.

Furmark, Tomas. (2000). Social Phobia, From Epidemiology to Brain Function. Uppsala University Press.

Fenichel, Otto. (1945). The Psychoanalytic Theory of Neurosis. W. W. Norton & Company.

Foer, Jonathan. (2005). Extremely Loud & Incredibly Close. Houghton Mifflin, Publisher.

Fredrickson, Barbara. (2011). Positivisms. One World Publications

Freud, S. (1916). Psychopathology of Everyday Life. Macmillan, Publisher.

Freud, S. (1930). General Introduction to Psychoanalysis. Horace Liveright, Publisher.

Freud, S. (1946). On Narcissism: An Introduction. Modern Library, Publisher.

Freud, S. (1959). Collected Papers. Basic Books, Publisher.

Fromm, E. (1980). The Heart of Man. Harper Collins, Publisher.

Fromm, E. (1994). Escape From Freedom. Farrar & Rinehart, Publisher.

Fromm, E. (2006) The Art of Loving. Harper & Brothers, Publisher.

Fisher, Helen. (1994). Anatomy of Love: The Nature and Chemistry of Romantic Love. Random House, Publisher.

Franklin, Victor. (2006). Man Search for Meaning. Beacon Press.

Gallagher, Sandra. (2015). The Art of Living. Penguin Random House, Publisher.

George, F. Will. (2010). Men at Work. Harper Collins Publisher.

Gray, John. (2012). Men are From Mars, Women are from Venus. Harper Paperbacks Publisher.

Gilbert, Ryle. (1949). The Concept of Mind. University of Chicago Press.

Gordon, James. (1988). Holistic Medicine. Chelsea House Publisher.

Grayson, Jonathon. (2004). Freedom from Obsessive Compulsive Disorder. Berkley Trade Publisher.

Haanel, F. Charles. (2007). Mental Chemistry. Filiquarian Publisher.

Hatfield, Elaine. (1993).Emotional Contagion. Cambridge University Press.

Horney, Karen. (1981). Neurosis and Human Growth: The Struggle towards Self- Realization. W.W. Norton & Company Publisher.

Hippocrates. (2006). Health Program: A Proven Guide to Healthful Living. Author Choice Publisher.

Hsin Hsin Ming. (2014). The Zen Understanding of Mind & Consciousness. Osho Media International.

Hood, Ralph, Hill, Peter, Spilka, Bernard. (2009). Psychology of Religion. The Guilford Press.

Hoffer, Eric. (2010). The True Believer. Harper Perennial Modern Classics.

Huxley, Aldous. (1932). Brave New World. Penguin Modern Classics.

Hume, David. (2003). A Treatise of Human Nature. Courier Corporation.

Hubel & Wilder. (1982). Spatial Frequency Selectivity of Cells in Macaque Visional Cortex. Visions Press vol.22. Pp545 to 559.

Ian, Stevenson, (1997). Where Reincarnation & Biology Intersect. Praeger Publisher.

Iacoboni, Marco. (2009). Mirroring People. Farrar, Straus, & Giroux, Publisher

James, William. (1985). Psychology Briefer Course. Harvard University Press Publisher.

Jung, Carl. (1912). Psychology of the Unconscious. Courier Corporation Publishing

Kahneman, Daniel. (2011). Thinking Fast and Slow. Farrar, Straus & Giroux, Publisher.

Kafaji, Talib. (2011). Inward Journey. Author House Publishers, Indiana.

Kafaji, Talib. (2011). The Psychology of the Arab. Author House Publishers, Indiana.

Kafaji, Talib. (2013). The Triumph over the Mediocre Self. Author House Publishers, Indiana.

Kafaji, Talib. (2014). Contemplative Thoughts in Human Nature. Author House Publisher, Indiana.

Kierkegaard, Soren. (1987). Either/Or Part 1. Princeton University Press.

Koestler, Arthur. (1967). The Ghost in the Machine. Arkanan Publisher.

Kant, Immanuel. (2008). Critique of Pure Reason. Penguin Classics.

Kehoe, John.(2007).Mind Power. Zoetic Books.

Kempermann, Gerd.(2011). Adult Neurogenesis. Publisher OUP, USA.

Klein, Stefan. (2002). The science of Happiness. Marlowe & Company Publisher.

Krishnamurti, J. (2009). Freedom from the Known. Harper San Francisco, New Edition.

Laing, R. D. (1965). The Divided Self: An Existential Study in Sanity and Madness. Penguin Books.

Langer, Ellen. (1999). Mindfulness. Da Capo Press Publisher.

Leuthardt, Eric. (2014). Red Devil 4, Tor Books Publisher.

Leaf, Caroline.(2015). Switch On Your Brain. Baker Books Publisher.

Livet, Benjamin. (1991). Maerket for Livet. Publisher Reitzel.

Lipton, Bruce. (2005). The Biology of Belief. Mountain of Love Publisher.

Lama, Dalai.(1998). Buddha, The Fourth Noble Truth.

Loftus, Elizabeth. (1996). The Myth of Repressed Memory. St. Martin's Griffin Publisher.

Lorenz, Koarad.(1974). On aggression. Mariner Books Publisher.

Martin, N. Seif. (1976). Defensive and Cognitive Styles. Publisher Ferkauf Graduate School of Humanities & Social Science.

Masaru, Emoto. (2011). The Hidden Message in Water. Simon & Schuster Publisher.

McKay, Mathew, Olaoire, Sean, Metzner, Ralph. (2013). WHY. New Harbinger Publisher.

Mackay, Charles. (2003). Extraordinary Delusions and Madness of Crowds. Hariman House Publisher.

Mc Neill, David. (1992). Hand and Mind; What Gestures Reveal about Thought. University of Chicago Press.

May, Rolla. (1969). Love & Will. W.W. Norton & Company.

Marx, Karl. (2000). Selected Writings. Oxford University Press.

Merzenich, Michael. (2013).Soft Wired. Parnassus Publisher.

Meltzoff, Andrew. (2000). The Scientist in the Crib. William Morrow Paperback.

Miller, Thomas. (2014). Investment. McGraw- Hill Education.

Navia, E. Luis. (2007). Socrates: A Life Examined. Prometheus Books.

Nietzsche, Friedrich. (2000). Basic Writings of Nietzsche. Modern Library, Publisher.

Nightingale, Earl. (1993).The Essence of Success. Publisher Nightingale Conant Corporation.

Nottebohm, Fernando. (1993). Hope for the New Neurology. New York Academy Science Publisher.

Oakley, David. (2014). Mind for Numbers, Tarcher Perigee Publisher.

Ofshe, Richard. (1996). Making Monsters False Memories. University of California Press.

Orwell, George. (1984). Animal Farm. Houghton Mifflin Harcourt Publisher.

Ornesh, Dean. (1999). Love and Survival: 8 Pathways to Intimacy and Health. William Morrow Paperbacks Publisher.

Palmer, R. Jeffry. (1984). Emergence. Spectra& Reissue Publisher

Plato. (2002). Five Dialogues. Hackett, Publisher.

Peter, J. Laurence. (2011). The Peter Principle: Why Things Always go Wrong. Harper Business Publisher.

Penfield, Wilder. (2015). Mystery of the Mind. Princeton University Press.

Pinker, Steven. (2009). How the Mind Works. W.W. Norton & Company.

Plutarch. (2012). Parallel Live. Start Publishing.

Renee, Descartes. (1984). Principles of Philosophy. Springer Science & Business Media.

Ricard, Matthieu. (2003). Happiness. Little Brown and Company Publisher

Robert, Brent. (1960). The Golden Book Chemistry. Golden Book Press.

Ropeik, David. (2010). How Risky Is It, Really: Why Our Fears Do Not Always Match the Facts. McGraw-Hill, Publisher.

Rousseau, Jean-Jacques. (1992). Discourse on the Origins of Inequality. Hackett, Publisher.

Rushton, Philippe. (1994). Race, Evolution, and Behavior: A Life History Perspective. Transactional Publishers.

Roger, Carl. (1980). A Way of Being. Mariner Books.

Sartre, Jean-Paul. (1989). No Exit and Three Other Plays. Vintage Reissue.

Sasson, Remez. (2007). Peace of Mind in Daily Life. Published by Remez Sasson.

Seligman, Martin. (2002). Authentic Happiness. Simon & Shuster Publisher.

Shapiro, Dan. (2016). Life is a Fork in the Road. The book is in the making.

Shaw, George Bernard. (2001). Man and Superman. Penguin Classics.

Spiegel, Herbert. (2004). Trance and Treatment: Clinical Uses of Hypnosis. American Psychiatric association.

Sir Swami Sarnna. (1963). Thought-Power. Publisher by the Divine Life Society.

Smith, T. Shawn. (2011). The User's Guide to the Human Mind. New Harbinger Publications.

Spinoza, Baruch. (1995). The Letter. Publisher Hackett Company.

Sperry, W. Roger. (1983). Science and Moral Priority. Columbia University Press.

Stanley, Jones. (2014). Abundant Living, Abingdon Press.

Turner & Greenough. (1998). Effects of Experience and Environment on the Developing and mature brain. Implication for Laboratory Animal Housing. [ILAR], journal.

T.H. Huxley. (1863). Man's Place in Nature. Publisher William & Norgate

Thompson, Fay. (2013). Azez Medicine. Billboard Press.

Tolstoy, Leo. (2008). War and Peace. Vintage Classics Press.

Tzu, Lao. (1990). Tao Te Ching. Harper Perennial Compact Edition.

Webster's New World Dictionary. (1957). The World Publishing Company.

Webley, Paul & Lea, Stephen. (2001). The Economic Psychology of Everyday Life. Psychology Press.

William Butler Yeats. (2013). The Collected Work of W. B. Yeats. Simon & Shuster Publisher.

Wilde, Oscar. (2003). Complete Works of Oscar Wilde. Collins, Collins. Classics Edition.

Wilson, Timothy. (2009). Social Psychology. Pearson Press.

Weinberger, Norman. (1992). Memory; organization and Locus of Change. Oxford University Press.

Zahavi, Dan. (2000). Exploring the Self. John Benjamin Publisher

Zimbardo, Philip. (2008). The Lucifer Effect: Understanding How Good People Turn Evil. Random House Publishers.

Printed in the United States
By Bookmasters